I GRADUATED...
NOW WHAT?

A POST-COLLEGE SURVIVAL GUIDE
TO HELP YOU NAVIGATE "THE REAL WORLD"

D0878643

Alicia Dupree

Cover and Interior Design: Dino Marino, www.dinomarno.com

Paperback ISBN: 978-0-9999023-0-1

eBook ISBN: 978-0-9999023-1-8

I Graduated...
Now What?

A post-college survival guide
to help you navigate The Real World

Alicia Dupree

To my father, John Granados,
who reminded me daily (and still does!)
that my potential is unlimited.

TABLE OF CONTENTS

INTRODUCTION..I

CHAPTER ONE: HOW DO I DECIDE WHERE TO LIVE?...............................1

CHAPTER TWO: HOW DO I FIND AN APARTMENT?..................................20

CHAPTER THREE: HOW DO I FIGURE OUT WHAT TYPE OF CAREER TO PURSUE?...........35

CHAPTER FOUR: HOW DO I LAND A GREAT JOB?...................................59

CHAPTER FIVE: HOW DO I GET AROUND?...84

CHAPTER SIX: HOW DO I MANAGE THE MONEY I'M MAKING?...............103

CHAPTER SEVEN: HOW DO I CUT BACK ON MY VARIABLE EXPENSES?...........120

CHAPTER EIGHT: HOW DO I STAY OUT OF (OR GET OUT OF) CREDIT CARD DEBT?...........138

CHAPTER NINE: HOW DO I FIND BALANCE IN LIFE?.............................161

PARTING THOUGHTS...190

ACKNOWLEDGEMENTS...192

BOOK RECOMMENDATIONS..195

APPENDIX...210

INTRODUCTION

Hey there new grad,

How are you feeling? Still a little hungover from the grad parties? A little relieved that the last final is over? A little nervous to see where your grades end up and what is in store for you? Maybe you're just happy that you're officially a graduate and ready to roll with whatever comes next. Either way, there's a lot of "unknowns" ahead of you, and while that can be exciting, it can also be a little scary too!

The thing is, your life is different now from the way it was before your commencement ceremony. Think back to the day you graduated. Then think about today. Do you feel any different? Aside from the diploma that you've received and the leftover excitement from all of the celebrating, is it really any different?

News flash—it is! Now that you're a college grad, you've become a member of a different group of people. You're no longer a college student, protected by the excuse that you're "figuring it out" or "finding yourself." Often, the expectation is that you should have found yourself by now. After all, you've had eight semesters (perhaps a few more) to do just that. Whether you like it or not, you've graduated into a new category of people. You're an adult in a different way than you were when you turned eighteen. For most people, this is the first time where the decisions you make can really impact your post-graduate life.

Up until now, you've probably had a relatively clear path. The details may be a bit different for you, but it probably went a little something like this: focus on high school enough to get decent grades, join some clubs so your college applications look passable, and then pick a college where you hope to spend the next four years. At some point while in school, you make decisions about where to live, whether or not to join Greek life or specific clubs, what major to choose, and whether or not you go to Cancun again or try a new location for spring break. True, you may pick a lousy roommate, switch your major, or wish you didn't drink so much at Señor Frog's. But, at the end of the day, most college graduates end up on relatively the same path. This path has been laid out for you by the universities and all of those who have graduated before you.

But now... now you can really screw up. The decisions you make from this point forward carry more weight, and if you get them wrong, the safety net you've been used to may not be there anymore. And if it is, it's paper thin. If you are forced to use it once, it may not be there if or when you need it the next time. Wait, are you even allowed to still ask your parents for help? You're supposed to be an "adult" now. But how do you know how to "adult" when you've had little real-life experience adulting? You've entered a weird in-between stage where you're ready to be on your own but still have a lot of learning to do. You don't need your parents in the same way that you did in high school, but perhaps you're not quite ready to make all of the decisions on your own. You may need to lean on them—but also want your space and independence. Navigating this gray area is a bit tricky. Know that you'll eventually land somewhere that feels comfortable. Until then, give yourself some grace until you get it right. Seemingly overnight, you're faced with making decisions around where you live, what you do for work, and how you stay in touch with friends who have moved all over the country and perhaps the world. You need to learn how to live on your own, balance a budget, buy a car, buy a house, and create a digital presence without damaging your real-life reputation.

And then there are the realities that hit you right in the gut, like the fact that a college degree used to hold more weight than it does now. It used to separate you from the rest. Now, it's just table stakes. It allows you to be on the same level as the other two million-ish graduates who will enter post-college life this year. Don't get me wrong; getting a degree is still an admirable feat. I want my kids to go to college. I have a degree and am proud of it. And I'm proud of you too! I am in no way discounting your degree. I am, however, letting you know that your degree is often just another box that can be checked on a job application. It won't ensure that you get the job. That's on you. But I want to help you get the job of your dreams.

On top of setting yourself apart from other graduates, you'll also need to figure out how to change society's perception of "Generation Z" and learn to work with the generations that have come before you (Millennials, Gen Xers, and Baby Boomers). The members of those prior generations will likely be the ones hiring you, and they may not understand your perspective and positions, as they have their own perspectives and positions. The great news is that they're faced with the same challenge: they're looking to learn how to work with you, as they know that the future employees they hire are different than them. Essentially, though, you share the same goal, even if it may not appear that way on the surface. You both want that job filled. They need someone to join their team and you, my friend, need a job!

THE DAY THIS BOOK WAS BORN

This book came about after a conversation with my dad on the day after my graduation when he asked me if I was ready. Ready? Ready for what?

"The real world," he said.

"No," I thought. "Of course not!"

I was excited, but was I actually prepared? I told him that I wished there was a post-college survival guide available, one that would help me navigate these uncharted waters.

He suggested, "Why don't you create one?" And so I did. You're reading it now! I hope that I can help you save time and learn from the hindsight of others. I have my story, but it's only one story. There are things I would do again and things I would definitely not do again. Let me start by saying that I'm not an expert in any of the areas that I'm going to talk about. Having admitted that, I've collected advice from experts in these areas and have compiled stories of success and failures from prior graduates. You will hear from people who have been out of school for twenty-four months and some who have been out of school for almost twenty-four years. You'll hear from people who went back to school right away and some who immediately entered corporate America and the "rat race" that you may have heard about. You'll hear from people who made smart financial decisions and some who made terrible ones. I was able to contribute a lot to this second category, sharing how I fully damaged my credit and worked my ass off to diligently repair it. You'll have to wait until chapter eight to read that story!

Not every part of this book will be relevant to you... at least not right now. My hope is that you use this the way it was intended: to pick up and put down when it's necessary. Already have a job lined up? Great, no need to spend time on the chapter around finding a job. But the sections on setting up 401ks and budgets may be perfect for you. And maybe you pick this back up when it's time to interview for a new job. Are you living on your own and cooking for yourself for the first time? If so, you may want to revisit the relevant chapters again and again until you find something that works for your lifestyle.

Perhaps it's a book you use and then gift to someone else; it would be great if you get to a point where you feel so good in all of these areas of your life that you can pass these insights on to someone who may be approaching graduation. Or maybe it's better suited for your friend who is still pretending he's in college and is crushing pitchers of beer on Tuesday nights while he waits for his "dream job" to land in his beer-soaked lap. Either way, use it as you want for as long as you want, until you have collected enough personal experience to write a book of your own. I want you to succeed. And thrive. And learn from some of the mistakes that those who came before you made and give yourself some grace when you stumble a bit in these coming years.

I loved college. Absolutely LOVED it. They were some of the best years of my life. But not *the* best; for me, post-college life has been even better. And I truly believe your "best" is yet to come!

Get out there; the world's waiting for you.

Alicia

Chapter One

HOW DO I DECIDE WHERE TO LIVE?

For most graduates, as your time in college ends, your college living arrangements also come to an end. If you decide to start a career in the same city your college is located, you may not need to move at all. Perhaps you're in a great place already and there's no need to look for a new setup. But for many, it's time to look for a new place to call home.

Choosing where to live is a significant decision involving many variables. The first question to answer is, do you already have a job? If so, excellent; you've got a good idea as to where you may live, geographically speaking.

What if the answer is, "No, I don't have a job yet"? Then ask yourself if you know where you'd like to work. If the answer is yes, do you move there and then start looking for a job once you're settled? What if you don't know where you'd like to settle? What if you're open to living in a few different cities, or anywhere at all? Where should you live while you search for employment?

Whether you've secured a job or not, the following are four popular options for post-college living arrangements:

1. Move where the job is, assuming you already have one.
2. Move to a new city of interest, and find a job once you get there.
3. Move back in with Mom and Dad.
4. Stay right where you are and begin a career there.

Let's explore each of those options in more detail.

1. MOVE WHERE THE JOB IS

If you already have a job—and that job requires you to be present in an office every day—then you can skip ahead to the next chapter and focus on finding the actual apartment or house that you'll call home for the near future. You'll also need to consider whether you will live on your own or seek out roommates. Perhaps there are friends, family, or acquaintances that are also looking to move to the city where you'll be working. Before you consider sharing your place with others, however, take a look at the questions on the upcoming pages to determine if having a roommate is the right move for you.

2. MOVE TO A NEW CITY

So you've always wanted to live in California but went to school in Virginia and are from Pennsylvania? No? Just me? I know I'm not alone here; as a college graduate, you've finally got the freedom to literally go anywhere. You can decide to see what it's like to live in Portland or Omaha or Miami or London. There are no limits to where you can go!

But, although there are *technically* no limits on where you can go, perhaps there are factors unique to you that you may want to consider. Each city offers its own advantages and disadvantages when you consider costs, job market, available industry, distance from friends/family, weather, etc. And each of these decisions is unique to the one deciding. For one person, Manhattan may be the most ideal place to live. For others, the thought of living there would be a complete nightmare. The small-town feel of Little Rock might be exactly what you're looking for, while others might think that's way too "small" for them.

One quick search on the Internet will reveal list after list of the "Top/Best Cities for (insert qualifier here)." You can find the "Top Cities for Graduates," "Top Cities for Singles," "Top Cities for Food," "Top Cities for Dogs"—anything. While perusing these lists is helpful, know that they're written from one person's perspective. You need to decide what's most important to you and then decide where to go from there.

The following are some of the more common factors people consider when deciding where to move/start a career:

- **Cost of living:** (includes housing costs, commute costs, taxes and other options): Look up how "affordable" it is to live in the locations you're considering. You may be paid a smaller salary for the same job in Dallas than you would if you took the same job in San Francisco, but how far does your money go? That extra $10k you make in San Francisco could be quickly gobbled up in the cost of living difference between the two cities. When all is said and done, you could actually make "less" in California than you would in Texas. Think about the cities you're considering: what's the average price of an apartment there? How much are state and local taxes? Does your potential state have sales tax? What about income tax? Saving the sales tax on every purchase you make and/or not paying taxes on your income (which we'll address in a later chapter) is very significant, especially when you track those savings over time.

- **Employment landscape:** While every city has a job market, some cities have a heavier focus on one industry over others. If you're in the technology space, San Francisco, Austin, and Seattle can be great places for you to settle. If you're in the biotech space, heading to San

Diego or Boston may be a good strategy for you. Want to live in Tulsa but want a job in finance? That's okay—it's possible—just know that there are far more finance jobs in New York City. Other careers such as nursing and teaching are far less geography-based since there are hospitals and schools everywhere.

- **Climate:** Your own personal definition of "good weather" is going to come into play here. San Diego is famous for its fantastic weather. I'm not sure how many people could argue the fact that it boasts one of the greatest climates in the country. However, some may prefer the dry, arid climate in Arizona. Or the snowy Colorado winters/springs, and with their comfortable summers, may be peak conditions for you. I love visiting Florida, but the year-round humidity wouldn't work for me (and certainly not my hair). To each their own here.

- **Distance from friends and family:** Going from the comfort of college and the proximity to friends who feel like family to a new city where you may not know anyone is a scary thought. You will want to see the loved ones that you've left behind, or the ones who have left you behind. How far away are you? Can you hop in a car and be there in a few hours? How much are flights back home to see friends and family? How far is the airport? Personally, I'm not picking a city based on its airport, but thinking about the frequency with which you'll use the airport to travel for work or pleasure is important. When I lived in San Diego, we were about fifteen minutes from the airport. Currently, I live less than thirty minutes from the Newark Airport. When my brother and his wife lived in a suburb of Atlanta, it sometimes took two hours to get the airport. This may not matter to some, but he often traveled for work and they hosted visitors regularly. Those one- to two-hour trips added up, and now, as they start to settle in St. Louis, it's become more critical for them to buy a house that's closer to the airport.

- **Support network:** At this point in your life, chances are you've got a few pockets of close friends. Friends from elementary and high school. Friends from college. Friends from sports teams you've been on and jobs that you've held. Family friends that you've grown up with. I am fortunate to have incredible friends, some of which have been in my life for almost thirty years! If you're in the same boat, I'm sure you'd find it extremely comforting to move to a location where at least some of those friends reside. If you choose to move to a new town/city where you don't know anyone, you may feel lonely. Having a friend (or even a friend of a friend) around could help with the transition.

When my two friends decided to go to law school one year after college, I told them I would go with them for a year or two if it was somewhere 'fun.' They chose San Diego and I was in even though I had never been to California. I left my job at a publishing company in New Jersey, with no job lined up. One month after I arrived, I secured an entry-level job making $12/hour as an assistant at a marketing firm, 40 miles from my apartment. It wasn't enough to pay my bills, but I worked hard, and quickly worked my way up in account management, eventually leading that department as VP of Marketing and Account Services, and making more money than I knew what to do with at that time. If I hadn't taken that job, I wouldn't have met my best friend, or my husband and probably would have left San Diego after about a year. I ended up living there for 17!"

- Jacki, The College of New Jersey, Class of 1999

- **Sociocultural factors:** This is another category that's going to be highly personal. What do you like to spend your time doing? If you're interested in outdoor sports and hiking, a major city with colder climates may not be the best option for you. You may do better with a more suburban or rural set up where hiking trails and outdoor activities are more prevalent. If you enjoy spending time and money dining and experiencing the arts and entertainment offerings, a metropolitan option is likely a better fit. As a music lover, being in Nashville or New Orleans may be an excellent environment for you.

Now that you've thought about some of the things to consider when searching for an area to call home, consider taking an approach that you may have used when deciding which college to attend. Start by writing a few cities that you're considering across the top of the table. Then list the six factors below in the order of personal importance on the left side of the table.

	NYC	SEATTLE	KANSAS CITY
COST	Bad	Fair	Good
JOBS	Good	Good	Fair
WEATHER	Fair	Bad	Fair
DISTANCE FROM HOME	Bad	Fair	Good
SUPPORT NETWORK	Bad	Fair	Good
CULTURE/SOCIAL SCENE	Good	Good	Fair

Then start filling in each box with "Bad, Fair, or Good," based on fact versus feeling as much as you can. For instance, it is a fact that NYC is one of the more expensive places to live in. It is a fact that if your family lives in California, NYC is a far distance from where you grew up. It is a fact that NYC has a strong culture and food/social scene. That being said, feelings do come into play somewhat. Here's where personal preferences start to bubble to the surface. For example, you may think the weather in NYC is bad because it snows a lot. Someone else may find the snow wonderful (it should be noted that most of those people who think this have never tried to get to work during a "wintry mix;" it's a complete shitshow). So you may choose to put "fair" or "bad" while someone else may say "good," but ultimately, it's your list. Fill it in however you want. Then, once it's all filled in, take a step back and see what the list reveals. In this case, assuming the order of the criteria is correct, Kansas City may be the best place for you to settle down. If cost is your main driver, followed by job opportunities, weather, and the distance from home, this could be a good choice for you. Following those same four criteria, NYC probably wouldn't be a great choice for you since the cost of living outweighs the number of available jobs. It's all relative, too; NYC definitely has more available jobs than most other cities, partly because it's bigger than most other cities and also has more people than most other cities. But remember that just because there are more jobs doesn't mean it's easier to get one. As of 2018, almost 8.4 million people live in NYC (according to the US Census), and an additional one million or so travel into the city each day. That's a lot of people trying to find (and keep!) their jobs. Make sure you're thinking through this one.

3. LIVE WITH MOM AND DAD

It used to be taboo to move home with mom and dad. Once you turned 18, you went to college and officially flew the coop. Over the past few years, though, there's been a trend of more and more graduates moving home, even for a little while. And maybe it's still a little taboo and not ideal, but it may be the right move for you. Don't discount this option without giving it some thought.

What are some pros? One, this is usually a financially-sound decision. Unless your parents are slumlords, they're not going to take advantage of your slight desperation. At least my parents didn't. They didn't charge for utilities. They didn't make me pay for groceries. Having said that, my "landlords" did charge me $250/month in rent during the six months I lived at home after college. Writing that $250 check is laughable now when my NYC rent a few years later was ten times as much as that. But I appreciated that they were getting me familiar with having to write a check on the first of each month. Regardless of the amount, paying rent got me in a good habit and forced me to start budgeting for that pending payment coming at the top of the following month. Another advantage of moving home was having home-cooked meals and quality time with my family. Although my parents didn't do my laundry, I was fortunate not to have to buy detergent or spend an afternoon waiting for my clothes to be cleaned in a laundromat. I was able to use their appliances free of charge. Plus, it was nice being around my high school friends who had stayed in the area or moved home with their parents after graduation.

I enjoyed being home at first, but as the months went on, I was yearning for the same freedom and flexibility that I had in college. The lack of that freedom is, in my opinion, one of the biggest challenges that comes with moving home. You were used to being on your own, coming and going as you please. Now you're forced to revert back to the rules of your parents' house that, out of sheer respect, you should follow. After all, your parents are letting you live there rent-free (or at a very reduced price). I'd imagine some rules won't apply to you now in the same way they applied to you while you were in high school, but at times you'll likely feel like you've taken a little step backward. It's definitely more badass to be fully independent and on your own right after you graduate, and there may be a bit of shame attached to making the decision to "move back home." I can understand that. But I think there's more shame in getting yourself into a bad situation that might have been avoided if you had returned home for a bit and taken your time to decide on your next move. For me, I knew I was moving from Pennsylvania to California within six months of graduating, so moving home for the short-term just made sense.

If you decide to go this route, one thing that really helps is sitting down with your parents and going over expectations. Maybe their "rules" are fewer than you expected. Perhaps all they want is for you to pick up the groceries every once in a while or check in when you get home each night, as my parents asked me to do. I found this odd, considering that for the past four years, they'd had no idea where I was and what time I came home. (Fast forward to now, as a parent, I totally understand the need to go to bed knowing that your children are safe.) When kids are away at school, it is an out-of-sight, out-of-mind thing for most parents. I never called them when I got in for the night; I just came and went as I pleased. Quite honestly, had texting/FaceTime been around when I was in college, some questionable (and potentially drunk) conversations may have occurred if I had to check in with my parents each night. At any rate, get clear on the expectations they have and how they want you to contribute in order to make it a successful living arrangement for all.

Depending on the relationship you have with your family, this could either be a great move for you or a challenging one. Even though it wasn't an ideal setup for either party in my case, looking back, it was absolutely the right move for me. Because I was a different person than when I'd left for college four years prior, I was able to recognize the beneficial nature of that setup. Since I'd moved out on my own and understood the magnitude of what living "on your own" means, I was all the more grateful. Oh, and it should be noted (because my mom will read this and be pissed if I don't mention it) she did give me back all the rent that I paid to her and my dad over the six months that I lived with them. The $1500 that they saved for me was a great cushion to kick-start my first few months on my own, when it was my name on the lease and my credit on the line. It should also be noted that this doesn't happen in real life. Your landlord cashes your checks and does not give the money back to you. Thanks again, Mom and Dad!

4. STAY LOCAL TO WHERE YOU WENT TO SCHOOL

If you went to college in or around a major metropolitan area, you might choose to stay there after graduation to begin your career locally. Often local employers will have connections with the career centers at nearby universities, and perhaps thanks to that, you were (or will be) able to find a job that doesn't require you to move. That's great! You're in a city you probably already know well. I would assume that you are at least somewhat familiar with the public transportation options. You probably know the local spots to get a cheap, healthy lunch as well as the not-so-healthy options that are especially tempting in the wee hours of the morning. It's also likely that others you know from school will take the same route as you, staying nearby to start working. This is very helpful if you decide to live with roommates. Having roommates that you know can be more comforting. Knowing them, however, is not a guarantee that they will be good roommates. Great friends don't always make great roommates, but they're not total strangers, and there's a lot to be said for that.

DO YOU WANT TO LIVE WITH ROOMMATES OR ON YOUR OWN?

Speaking of roommates, is having a roommate the best move for you? Before you begin your search and commit to living with someone, think of the following:

1. Do you like living with other people?
2. Can you afford to live on your own?
3. Do you know anyone in the area where you will be living? If not, are you comfortable living with a random stranger?

4. What did you like/dislike about living with roommates in college?

5. Do you know yourself well enough to know what it's like to live with YOU? What type of roommate are you?

LIVING SOLO

When you ask yourself the questions above, you may decide that living with someone just isn't in the cards for you. As with all decisions waiting for you post-graduation, and throughout your whole life, there are some advantages and disadvantages that accompany this decision.

If you decide to live on your own, you are in total control of your living space. Your mess is your mess. If you leave a clean apartment in the morning, you will come back to a clean apartment at night. You can have guests stay with you for as long as you'd like, without having to clear it with someone else. You also don't need to deal with a roommate's guests or significant other coming over and acting as a third wheel. There's no roommate drama, and you have ultimate independence.

But this independence comes with a price tag. It's generally more expensive to live on your own. The cost of a studio or one-bedroom is typically less than most two-bedroom apartments, but you aren't splitting utilities with anyone. Electric, cable, water, gas, Internet—all of those expenses are on you. Also on you? All of the chores needed to maintain an apartment. With roommates, maybe one cooks and the other cleans. Or one cleans the bathroom one weekend and the other takes the next week. But when it's just your place, you're taking care of all of the cleaning. You also don't have someone to lean on if you're in a jam and locked out of your place or just want someone to talk to when you get home. It can be lonely and isolating or perfectly calm and quiet; it's all based on how you look at the situation and what your preferences are.

The following are what some recent graduates had to say about living alone:

> *After living at home for a year, I moved into my own apartment and lived there by myself for two years. That was such a peaceful time. I really enjoyed the independence. That's also when I became very conscious about keeping things orderly. Anything out of place drove me crazy, and I found joy in cleaning. Some repair things were difficult, such as hanging lights and placing and removing my window AC units, but my nextdoor neighbor helped me out a lot. I found young apartment neighbors were actually very kind to one another."*
>
> - Allyson, Muhlenberg College, Class of 2004

> *I should have lived at home longer to save more money before moving out on my own. I accrued credit card debt (all of which has been paid off for several years now) but didn't truly understand what a good credit rate was. I wanted to be on my own and didn't feel comfortable consulting my parents to truly understand what a good rate looked like."*
>
> - Kendra, James Madison University, Class of 2005

> *I lived on my own in a tiny apartment in Marietta, PA. Rent was $450 per month. It worked because it was my own. My mess. My space. I learned to pay bills and be responsible on my own. I lived on my own for four years before I was married and then moved in with my husband."*
>
> - Elyse, York College, Class of 2003

YOU DEFINITELY WANT (OR NEED!) A ROOMMATE

College was my first experience living with a roommate, if you don't count my parents and three brothers. And while it worked out okay, there was a lot to be learned during that first experience. Once I started making friends and building relationships, finding roommates for sophomore through senior year was fun! Finding someone to live with didn't seem as scary because they were known entities. But do all great friends make great roommates? Of course not! My old (and current!) roommates will tell you that I'm messy. I leave "Alicia tracks" wherever I go. Sometimes I forget to close a cabinet after I use it, and my signature move is letting pans "soak" in the sink overnight, secretly hoping that someone else will end up cleaning them. Whether it's someone's clutter, the hours they keep, the friends they have over, or the shows they're into, there are a lot of potential annoyances waiting to be discovered with a new roommate, even when that person is one of your closest friends. But imagine going to a new city, where you know no one, and having to find a roommate while anticipating all of those annoyances. That happens to many, which we will talk more about in the next section.

There was one year where I did have roommates, which was hard and also a learning process because you're basically sharing a space with other independent people who do things their own way. I think the greatest lesson I learned from this experience was that you can't place expectations on others."

- Brilynn, NYIT, Class of 2009

> " *I lived at home for about three months before moving to Baltimore with a friend. It worked that we were both new to the city and spent a ton of time exploring together.*"
>
> - Stacy, Slippery Rock University, Class of 2004

If you stay local to your college, chances are that other graduates will decide to do the same. Some may be in need of roommates. Plus, it's nice to have some familiar faces around. The fact that so many people from your alma mater may be local can also be a drawback, too. Staying in the same social circles after graduation can hinder your growth if you don't ever expand that circle. If you are closed to the idea of forming friendships with people you have yet to meet, you'll be missing out on a world of fun. Some of my closest friends now are people that I met post-college, and I couldn't imagine my world without them.

With that in mind, another option includes moving to a nearby city but living on your own and/or finding new roommates. This might allow you to have the best of both worlds: a familiar environment with local friends as well as exposure to a new group of people with unique interests and their own experiences and backgrounds. In gathering feedback and experiences for this book, I found that, when given the chance, most people opt to live with people they know. Even if there are drawbacks, the "devil you know" is often better than the rando that you meet online.

After college, I went to dental school and roomed with another dental student. We didn't know each other at all but ended up becoming great friends. I will actually be a groomsman in his wedding this year! It was also really helpful to live with someone who was going through the same difficult school schedule, and we helped to keep each other accountable."

- Preston, University of Texas at Austin, Class of 2009

I temporarily lived with a girl who was much younger than I was whom I had only met briefly, and it was an awful experience. I chose that option because it was inexpensive and convenient, but I wish I could have seen how she lived before committing to having her as a roommate. It is important to get to know the people you will be living with a bit and have a connection with them so you can feel comfortable in your own home."

- Melissa, University of Arizona, Class of 2006

LIVING WITH YOUR SIBLINGS OR SIGNIFICANT OTHER

Sometimes the idea of moving in with your current flame or a family member outside of your mom and dad can seem like a good play. And it is. Sometimes. Or it's not. Sometimes.

If you're considering moving in with your boyfriend or girlfriend, know that your relationship is about to shift as a result. It may get better, and it may get worse. But the dynamics will certainly shift, and you'll be able to learn a lot about them once they become your roommate. You'll get a sneak peek of what it's like to be around them all the time, and you'll be forced to address any problems that arise because you won't have your own places to retreat back to after a big argument. But what happens if you decide to call it quits? Then you're potentially stuck in a lease you might be unable to afford alone or suddenly finding yourself without a place to live. It happens all the time, but people survive. You will too. But it's something to keep in mind when making this decision.

> *I lived in an apartment with my boyfriend of a few years, which worked well until we broke up. He moved out, so I was stuck with paying the rent by myself. I had to break the lease and move in with friends."*
>
> - Portia, Florida Atlantic University, Class of 2002.

> *I moved to West Hollywood, CA, with a boyfriend. It was a challenge, moving to a city where I knew no one, did not have a car, did not have a job, and was most certainly not a celebrity. And the relationship definitely did not last. But what worked is I learned how to navigate public transportation, discovered how to find a job, and learned how independent I could be in the world, which set me up for success later."*
>
> - Tricia, Boston University, Class of 1998

> *After college, my now-husband and I lived together in a townhouse. The first year of living together, we wanted to kill each other; I think that's just natural growing pains. Learning each other's habits, schedules, weird pet peeves, etc."*
>
> - Taylor, University of Kansas, Class of 2015

Spent the summer at home before moving to CA, where my college boyfriend and I rented an apartment with friends. It worked, until it didn't... ha!"

- Nikki, James Madison University, Class of 2005

The same goes for living with family. Maybe you have a sibling who's a few years older than you and living in the city where you want to live. You've lived with them before, back before you went to college. But they are in a different life stage now. If they're a few years ahead of you, maybe they're making more money than you are. Sometimes their standard of living is higher than yours, and their habits are different than you remember. Chances are that you're close to your sibling if you're considering living together. That may mean that there are fewer boundaries between you, and a fight between the two of you can impact your entire family. But the trust factor with family is probably higher than it is with a roommate, especially one that you don't know before signing a lease. The years following college can be scary, especially if you're moving to an unfamiliar area. Having a piece of home with you as a roommate could help with the transition into a new stage of life. Think back to how the two of you were before college. If you had a great relationship then and feel like you have a great relationship now, this could be a wonderful move for you.

I lived with my sister in NYC, and my parents helped to subsidize my rent. It was hard because my sister's lifestyle and paycheck were much more extravagant than mine! I found I got into a lot of debt early on in my NYC days. I don't really know how I would have done it differently and honestly don't regret it, but I was definitely living beyond my means (as most people in NYC are, I believe!)."

- Mary-Paige, James Madison University, Class of 2004

Living with family can be good and bad because there is that level of comfortability, but sometimes there's also a lack of respect. I'm just grateful to have been able to hit a point of personal growth with my sister at the same time so that we could progress forward as great roommates."

- Brilynn, NYIT, Class of 2009

There is a lot to consider when deciding your first step after school. Sometimes all of the options and flexibility are overwhelming. If you had fewer choices, you wouldn't need to weigh these options so much because you'd have fewer to sort through. But know that this step is temporary. I'm sure it's happened, but I know exactly zero people who are currently living in the place they first lived right out of school. You can always move apartments, move cities, change jobs, find new roommates; know that even if it doesn't work out, it'll all be okay. You won't truly know if you made the right call until you're actually in the throes of that decision, so do your best, make the call that feels right at the time, and allow yourself some patience and grace if you get it wrong.

Key takeaways:

1. IF YOU DON'T ALREADY HAVE A LIVING SITUATION CONFIRMED, YOU'VE GOT FOUR MAIN OPTIONS:

   1. MOVE WHERE THE JOB IS

   2. MOVE WHERE YOU WANT AND THEN FIND A JOB

   3. HEAD BACK TO YOUR HOMETOWN (WITH OR WITHOUT A JOB)

   4. START WORKING IN THE CITY WHERE YOU WENT TO SCHOOL

2. DECIDE WHETHER OR NOT YOU WANT A ROOMMATE AND DETERMINE IF YOU'RE A GOOD ROOMMATE YOURSELF.

3. WHEN CONSIDERING A MOVE TO A NEW CITY, THINK ABOUT THE FOLLOWING BEFORE MAKING A DECISION:

   - COST OF LIVING

   - EMPLOYMENT LANDSCAPE

   - CLIMATE

   - DISTANCE FROM FRIENDS, FAMILY, AND A SUPPORT NETWORK

   - CULTURE OF THE TOWN/CITY.

   WEIGH THE IMPORTANCE OF ALL OF THESE FACTORS AND START NARROWING DOWN YOUR OPTIONS FROM THERE.

Chapter Two

HOW DO I FIND AN APARTMENT?

If you made it past the last chapter and are set on a geographic location in which you want to establish some roots, it's time to find a place to live. Perhaps you're in a spot to buy a house; if, after weighing all of the pros and cons that come along with homeownership, that's the route you decide go, this chapter won't be relevant. Feel free to skip ahead and come back to these pages if you decide to rent a place at some point in the future. That being said—and I'm making an assumption here—I think it's likely that most graduates won't be ready for homeownership right after college and are more comfortable renting a place for a while as they settle into post-college life.

But where do you even begin? If you've already found a job (which is often needed before you can secure an apartment), you can use it as a starting point. Where is the job located? How long do you want your commute to be? Where are the "best" neighborhoods to live in your city or town? Neighborhoods that are packed with restaurants, bars, shops, and similar establishments generally come with a higher price tag on their rentals. It's a supply and demand issue: the more coveted the location, the more a landlord can charge their tenants. You may decide that you're good with being a quick ride away from that "cool place to live" and grab an apartment just outside of town that's a little more affordable.

THE SEARCH PROCESS

Before you begin your search, make sure you figure out your rental budget as well as have your list of "must-haves" handy. Think about how much you can spend on just the rental portion of your living expenses. Narrow your search to apartments that are in that range. Share that range with your broker (if you're using one) and don't even walk into any apartments that are out of your range. Chances are they'll be the nicest ones you see (spoiler alert: that's why they're more expensive), and then you'll compare all other apartments to that one and may be disappointed with what your price range yields. If you walk into one and fall in love with it, there's a chance you may make an emotional decision and be stretched financially before you even move. If you're doing an online search, make the high end of your range the "maximum" and hold to that.

Unsure of how much to spend on an apartment? A standard rule of thumb is to spend no more than 30 percent of your income on rent and associated monthly costs like utilities, parking, condo or community fees, etc.). At 30 percent, you are considered "rent burdened," and if it creeps north of 60 percent, you are considered extremely rent burdened. If you're in a major city, it may be difficult to stick to this 30 percent rule and get a place that you really like. For example, let's assume you have a job that pays you $40,000 a year. (Note: this is not what you take home, by the way... we'll talk more about that in later chapters. But for now, let's use this number.) When you divide that annual salary by 12, that's $3,333/month in income. Using the above percentage as a guide, you should be spending no more than $1,111 on rent and the corresponding costs listed above.

One way to get that monthly cost down is by adding a roommate or two. But remember, that means more people sharing your space. More people using your kitchen and bathrooms. More people having the last scoop of your peanut butter or polishing off the ice cream you had stashed away to help you heal from a shitty day at work. There are often limits on the number of people that can share one space, so you can't keep adding people in order to decrease your portion of that monthly payment. Eventually, you'll need more bedrooms, which means a bigger space, which means a higher rent payment, and while the per-person amount may decrease—suddenly you're back to dorm life again. That may not be ideal for you, so weigh the pros and cons of roommate living and decide if the potential cost savings are worth the additional people sharing your address.

IS IT OKAY TO GO OVER BUDGET IF YOU SEE A PLACE YOU REALLY LOVE?

Not sticking to your maximum rental range can be a slippery slope. Suddenly the $1,111 maximum becomes $1,250. And then you see a place for $1,300 and start thinking about how you can make that work. And then you see another place for $1,350. On paper, it may not look like that much more, but month after month, that extra $75, $100, or $150 month will be felt. Now, if there are other items included in your monthly rent that you'd otherwise be paying for, the extra monthly rent may be worth it for you. Understand what is included. Is there a gym in the building? Instead of paying $50 - $100 for a membership elsewhere, perhaps you can afford paying that much more per month for this place. Are any utilities included in rent? Heat/trash/water/sewer/electric/garbage are all possible utilities you have to pay on top of your rent. If your landlord includes some of these in your monthly payment, you may be able to afford a higher monthly rent.

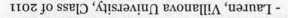

> *I didn't realize how much cable and electric would be on top of my rent!"*
>
> - Lauren, Villanova University, Class of 2011

You also want to consider what the apartment itself includes. How many bedrooms and bathrooms does it have? What does the kitchen look like? Do you think you'd actually use it to cook at home, or is it the type of kitchen that motivates you to order take-out? What types of amenities are included? Is there a great common area with a grill and a pool? This may mean you stay home on some weekends versus going out and spending money on food and entertainment at someone else's pool. This all needs to be factored into your price range.

Last but not least, when you head out at night or on the weekends, can you walk to places, or will you either need to drive and pay for parking or take an Uber or Lyft? If you are going to be working from home, getting a second bedroom that can be used as an office or paying a premium for a bit more living space could be worth it to you. If you're saving a couple of hundred dollars in transportation costs by not going into the office, could you pay $100 more for rent and have a more comfortable working environment at home? Ideally, you stick to your budget, but when faced with the option of a slightly over-budget rental, keep these factors in mind and then make the decision that is best for you.

IN WHICH SECTION OF TOWN/NEIGHBORHOOD DO YOU WANT TO LIVE?

If you already have a job, think about your commute time. On a Monday morning during rush hour, use Waze or Google Maps to see how long it would take to go from your potential apartment to your office. Do the same thing around 5:30 or 6:00 at night to see what the drive home is like. An extra few miles could add fifteen more minutes to your drive. That's thirty minutes each day, or two-and-a-half hours during the workweek. Is public transportation an option? If so, calculate the time it takes you to walk/drive to the train or bus. Then look at the schedules of those trains or buses and see what the door-to-door time is for that option.

If you don't have a job and you are forced to secure an apartment now, you won't be able to calculate commute times for a specific job. You can, however, look at your location compared to different areas of the city where jobs are concentrated. Do a search for jobs online and notice where some of your potential employers are located. Pull out a map and see where apartments in your price range are in relation to those micro-markets. Is it an exact science? No. But at least you're not going in completely blind. If at all possible, wait until you have a job to secure a place to live so that you can be well aware of what your daily commute will be. After the time actually spent at work, traveling to and from the office could possibly be the most time you spend on something each day!

Additionally, how far are you from things like a grocery store, pharmacy, coffee shop, restaurants, etc.? Can you walk to any of these places? If you don't have access to a gym with your rental, is there one nearby? What about a nice park for your morning runs? If you're unfamiliar with the area you're thinking about calling home, spend an afternoon there and try it on for size. Have lunch at a restaurant nearby. Grab a drink and a snack at a local coffee shop. Take a walk in that park you drove past in between looking at apartments. You have to picture yourself living here. You'll spend your days and nights, weekdays and weekends here for probably a year or more of your life. Do not skip this step!

WHAT'S PARKING LIKE?

If you have a car, where will you park it? Ideally, you have a reserved space or a driveway that's all yours, but if not, where will you park? Friends of mine who didn't consider this at first would spend the first ten minutes of each day walking to their car, and then after work circle around and around looking for a spot to park. Not how I'd like to spend my time but hey, to each their own. If you're in a metropolitan area, sometimes you will be charged a fee in order to have a parking spot, so again, make sure you take this into consideration when calculating what you can and cannot afford. Some cities offer abundant street parking but be sure to be mindful of all of the unique parking rules you may encounter. Ignoring this may cause you to accumulate expensive fines when you forgot about the street sweeping rules or parked too close to a fire hydrant (even though it was the only spot, and it was late, and it was cold, and you just wanted to get home in time for *The Bachelor*)?

 If you live in a city, be mindful of street cleaning and parking meters; it gets expensive!"

- Nikki, James Madison University, Class of 2005

In major metropolitan cities, you may opt for public transportation versus having a car in the city. In this case, you want to know how long it's going to take you to walk, skip, or run to the nearest bus, train, subway, etc.

CAN YOUR PETS LIVE THERE TOO?

If one of your roommates has four legs, you need to include pet-friendly listings in your search. Many places do not allow pets, and those that do usually require some sort of "pet deposit." Make your pet status clear when working with a broker or when searching on your own so you're only looking at places that will allow your furry friend to shack up with you. It would be a shame for you to fall in love with a place only to realize that you can't bring your pet along. Once you identify the options that allow pets, you need to determine if they fit your lifestyle. If you have a dog that will need to be taken outside regularly but you're out of the house for work from 6 a.m. until 6 p.m., who will let him out? Living in a high-rise may pose a problem, unless you plan on giving your dog walker a key and paying for them to swing by a few times a day. Maybe renting a single-family home with a doggy door and a backyard makes more sense for you? There's no right or wrong answer, just something to consider so you're not kicking yourself after the fact when you may be locked into a lease.

HOW'S THE APARTMENT AND SURROUNDING AREA AT NIGHT?

Most of the time, you view apartments during the day, which makes sense. You want to see how much light comes into the place and accurately get a look at all of the amenities and outdoor spaces you'll have access to if you were to become a tenant there. But what happens when the sun goes down? Is it a party scene and super loud, or is it just as quiet as during the day? Do you get that eerie feeling that makes you look over your shoulder every few steps? This is especially important if you'll be working later and coming home after the sun has gone down. If so, you want to get a good look at the surroundings at night. How well-lit is it? Where would you park, and what's the walk back to your place like? This isn't to scare you; it's just another thing to think about so you can be as informed as possible when deciding where to live.

> *I moved from the Midwest out to California and found a place called "Paradise Gardens" which looked amazing online. When we showed up ready to move in, everything in a 10 mile radius was completely run down and you couldn't even go inside of a gas station without encountering bulletproof glass. My apartment on the inside was nice. I just couldn't be outside without being in my car. Needless to say, all of the best parts of the apartment were featured online and they failed to mention any of the not-so-great features. I had already committed to a lease but moved out as soon as I could. Lesson learned!"*
>
> - Shalon, Ball State University, Class of 2003

HOW LONG IS THE RENTAL?

Part of your search should include a lease term that fits your situation. If you're currently living in Baltimore without a job but are applying to jobs in five other cities, I wouldn't commit to a long lease. Perhaps a month-to-month option would make more sense for you. You'd likely pay a bit more for this flexibility, but the flexibility might be something you need right now. And when you factor in the costs associated with potentially breaking the lease early, it may be a no-brainer to pay a bit more in the short term while you figure out your next move. This could also be a good option if you're in a new city. Perhaps a short sublease would work for you. It can act as a solid landing spot while you take a month or so to get more familiar with the city and answer important questions, like how's the commute? What's the neighborhood like? Where do you find yourself spending the most time? If it's close to where you are, then you can commit to a longer lease in the same area. But what happens if you quickly realize that the commute is far worse than you thought? In that case, at least it's a temporary setup, and you're now able to relocate to a better environment for you.

What happens if you land the job of your dreams that will force you to move? In many cases, you can speak with the person providing you with the job offer and see if there is any assistance they can provide, especially if relocation is an option.

A few years into my role at my former company, I had an opportunity to relocate but had six months left on my current lease. I made my leadership team aware of this, and they agreed to cover the $5k that I would have had to pay to end the lease early. Had I been too afraid to ask, I would have been on the hook for that amount. But you also can't assume that the company is going to absorb that cost. You need to bust out a calculator and start doing some math to determine if the new job that you're going for is worth it. Will you make more? Will you make the same or less but move to a market with a lower cost of living?

Perhaps you'll realize it makes sense to just eat the cost to break the lease, and it will all have been worth it in the end.

CAN YOU GET ANY INSIDER INFORMATION?

It may not always be possible, but if you can, do your best to talk to people who live in the building and/or in the area. Through conversation, try to uncover some unforeseen challenges that may come up regarding noise levels, timeliness of landlord responses, traffic patterns, etc. When you need a repair, how quickly does the landlord address it? Is there someone on the third floor who likes to rollerblade through his apartment in the middle of the night? Or does the woman living next to you have 21,489 cats? These are all things that you'd probably unhappily uncover once you've already committed to parking yourself in that apartment for a pre-defined amount of time. Any insight you can get ahead of time will be valuable. Social media could be a good tool for this "investigation" as well. Throwing up a post or tweet asking if anyone has lived in "x" neighborhood in "x" city or in a particular building in the past may yield some great insight. You might be surprised at what you find!

SHOULD YOU ENLIST THE HELP OF A BROKER?

In many cities, apartment complexes and independent landlords use a broker to help identify and rent out apartments. In cities like NYC and San Francisco, it feels almost impossible to land a great apartment without using a broker. Doing so will save you time and effort navigating the complex rental worlds of both of those cities... but it will cost you. Probably more that you think. In NYC, the typical broker commission is 15 percent of the annual rent. So, that $2,100/month apartment on the Upper East Side will require a $3,780 broker fee. That's paid by you. And you'll need the first and last months' rent as well. All of this is due before you get the keys. So suddenly that $2,100 apartment which seemed like a steal is now costing you $7,980 that first month. (Still want to live in NYC?)

Sometimes the landlord will pay for the broker if they are having trouble renting the place and they need help to find a tenant. In other cities (such as Chicago and Austin), the broker fee is paid by the apartment complex, and sometimes no broker fee exists at all. What does your city's rental market look like? Take a look at some online resources and get a good understanding of this before seeing your first apartment. Most cities don't require a broker to secure a lease, but in the event you're in one where a broker is recommended or almost "required," make sure you know what you're dealing with.

SECURING THE APARTMENT

While you're busy picking apart different features of the apartments you've toured, you're being picked apart by the people who have the vacancies. Landlords and property managers are interviewing you and seeking as much information as possible to determine your viability as a renter. Treat a meeting with a broker, property manager, or landlord like an interview. Also, assume they have already run your name across various social media sites to see what they can uncover. Be mindful of how you dress and how you present yourself. Do you need to show up in a suit or prom dress? No. Not necessary. But generally, you're not the only one interested in the open apartment, so it's best to assume that the landlord will be meeting with several potential tenants and present yourself well during those encounters. Take a look in the mirror and ask yourself, "Would I rent to me?" Do you look like you have your shit together? Do you look like you are responsible enough to pay your rent on time? Right, wrong, or indifferent, this impression matters, and it may factor into their decision to rent the apartment to you or not.

Aside from how you present yourself, landlords will also need to get a glimpse of your financial history. Often you'll be charged an application fee and sometimes that includes a fee to run your credit. Most of the time these fees aren't more than $50 each, which is nominal in the long run, but if you're applying to many apartments, these fees can add up quickly. You should also consider pulling your own credit report ahead of time to find out what they will. This way, if there are any issues that you can correct ahead of time, you'll have a chance to do it and you won't be blindsided by an error while you're in the midst of being considered for the apartment of your dreams. This error may be a deal-breaker, and it will be incredibly frustrating if you missed an opportunity to address it.

SIGNING THE LEASE

Once you've found an apartment you want to call your own, and your application for that apartment has been accepted, there's one more step you need to take before you officially call it "yours." You've got to sign the lease to make it official. This may be the first time you're signing a contract on your own, and the sheer number of pages—along with the language found on those pages—may be a bit overwhelming. Many times, landlords use a "standard" lease, but even though they are familiar with the terms, you may not be. If you need help understanding what you're signing, do not be afraid to ask.

THINGS TO LOOK OUT FOR IN A LEASE:

1. The current state of the apartment: Make sure that any/ all damage is documented before officially occupying the residence. Whip out your phone and take a video of how the apartment looks before calling it your own. Understand what your security deposit will cover and what constitutes normal "wear and tear." Some holes in the wall that resulted from hanging pictures may be no big deal. But needing to paint a wall, replace a carpet, or repair the hole you punched in the wall when your team lost game seven in the World Series? That you'll have to pay for.

2. How often can the landlord enter your apartment unannounced? They're going to have to come in for specific reasons, and sometimes it may be helpful for them to meet a repairman there, etc. But you want to know how often and how much notice must be given before they just show up. No one wants their landlord busting in while they're in the middle of an intense make-out session with that guy or girl from the bar.

3. Who is paying for what? Repairs? Utilities? Lawn maintenance? Snow removal? Pest control? Parking? If you are renting in a high-rise, you may not need to worry about things like lawn maintenance, snow removal, etc. But if you're renting a home or a room in a home, then what? Is the grass slowly becoming a jungle? And are you expected to shovel the whole driveway before heading into work if/when you get hit with a ton of snow? And pest control—get excited about this one! Even the cleanest apartments get bugs, especially during warmer months; it just happens. And it's gross. Who's paying for the exterminator, and how often does that lovely person come around to proactively prevent little critters from trying to bunk up with you? Do you have a designated parking spot? If so, is it included in the lease, or are you paying for it on your own? Know all of this before signing the lease and committing to the apartment.

4. How can you break the lease? Depending on the formality of the lease terms, you could see anything from no penalty to a massive one. No one can predict the future, but you can do your best to plan for it. If you know when you sign a lease that you have a job you love and plan on being in one place for the immediate future, it's safe to rent for a year, which is a very standard lease term. Some leases have you locked in for the full term, so if you had a one-year lease and wanted to break it after seven months, you may be on the hook for the remaining five months of rent, regardless of why you're canceling. Some landlords may charge you one month's rent and

keep your security deposit. Others are more flexible, especially if you assist in finding the next tenants. Please understand the terms of the lease you're about to sign. Everything is negotiable, so if the terms are unfavorable to you, feel free to ask about changes. Having said that, be aware of the competitive landscape of the rental market in your area. If you're one of ten people vying for one apartment, and you're asking about flexibility in lease terms, the landlord may opt for a tenant who appears more committed to a longer length of time. From their perspective, their goal is to have that place rented consistently, and although it may feel personal to you, it's business to them. And if there's a more attractive renter out there, they'll go with him or her.

RENTERS INSURANCE

One thing that you may not have needed to explore up until this point is renters insurance, which is exactly what it sounds like: an insurance policy that protects all of your personal belongings in your rental property (apartment, house, condo, etc.). Renters insurance can cover clothing, electronics, silverware, phones, military equipment, jewelry, fine art, bicycles, cameras, coins, computers, furniture, guns, music equipment, appliances, and a host of other items. Depending on your policy, your items are covered if damaged in a variety of situations, including fire, lightning, flood and water, windstorms or hail, collapse of building, vandalism and theft, freezing, and falling objects. Additionally, one of the great features about rental insurance is that it covers your "stuff" anywhere your "stuff" goes: in storage, your car, on a trip, anywhere.

As with car and health insurance, there are many types of policies available, and the prices for each policy vary depending on what they provide and the coverage offered. As you might suspect, the more coverage you request, the more you'll pay in an annual premium. USAA Insurance Company estimates that the average amount of coverage needed for a two-bedroom apartment begins at $20,000. They suggest creating an inventory of your personal belongings to help you determine how much coverage you need. Additionally, some landlords require that you have some sort of liability coverage before moving in, and these levels depend on your risk level for being held liable for injury or damages. For example, if you have pets or live with roommates, your risk level is higher than if you live alone.

As with all insurance, you are paying a premium for something that you hope you don't ever have to use. It's like having health insurance for normal check-ups and preventative care and hoping that you really don't need to call upon it for some catastrophic sickness or injury. But when you break your arm trying to reenact a move that you used to be able to do on a skate-board, you will be happy you have it. The same goes for renters insurance. It may feel like a bit of a waste of money, but in the event your items get damaged, you'll be happy that you have it.

Remember, while you can't predict the future, you can gather a ton of information ahead of time in order to make an educated decision. And if you get it wrong, it's okay. An apartment is a temporary situation; that's the beauty of renting. All leases come to an end, and although it may cost you, if it isn't working, you have the ability to break the contract. Aside from your place of employment, you'll likely spend most of your waking (and sleeping!) hours in your apartment/house/condo. Do your best to find one that matches all of your needs and most, if not all, of your wants.

Key Takeaways:

1. ESTABLISH A RENTAL BUDGET AND AIM TO KEEP IT AROUND 30 PERCENT OF YOUR MONTHLY INCOME.

2. IF YOU GO OVER BUDGET ON RENT, FACTOR IN INCLUDED AMENITIES (SUCH AS UTILITIES, USE OF GYM AND POOL, PARKING SPOT, ETC.) THAT MAY OTHERWISE BE ADDITIONAL MONTHLY EXPENSES.

3. BEFORE RENTING, MAP OUT YOUR COMMUTE DURING RUSH HOUR AND SEE HOW LONG IT WILL TAKE YOU TO GET TO AND FROM WORK DURING PEAK TIMES.

4. BE SURE TO FACTOR OTHER THINGS INTO YOUR DECISION: PARKING, PETS, NEARBY STORES AND RESTAURANTS, AND THE AREA SURROUNDING THE APARTMENT DURING THE DAY AND AT NIGHT.

5. DECIDE IF A SHORT-TERM RENTAL, ALTHOUGH USUALLY MORE MONEY PER MONTH, MIGHT MAKE MORE SENSE FOR YOUR LIFESTYLE AND CURRENT SITUATION.

6. IN URBAN AREAS, WEIGH THE PROS AND CONS OF ENLISTING THE HELP OF A BROKER TO AID IN YOUR SEARCH.

7. BEFORE SIGNING THE LEASE, MAKE SURE YOU UNDERSTAND ALL THE TERMS INCLUDED IN THE CONTRACT. MAKE SURE THAT THE LEASE DOCUMENTS THE CURRENT STATE OF THE APARTMENT UPON RENTAL, WHAT PAYMENTS YOU'RE RESPONSIBLE FOR, AND ANY PENALTIES ASSOCIATED WITH BREAKING THE LEASE EARLY.

8. YOU MAY BE REQUIRED TO PURCHASE RENTERS INSURANCE BEFORE OFFICIALLY MOVING INTO THE APARTMENT. IF YOU'RE NOT REQUIRED TO PURCHASE IT BY THE LANDLORD, YOU MAY WANT TO CONSIDER IT FOR YOUR OWN BENEFIT.

Chapter Three

HOW DO I FIGURE OUT WHAT TYPE OF CAREER TO PURSUE?

Now that you've graduated, you have to do something with your time; hopefully, that "something" brings in an income that will support both your necessities (food, rent, utilities, etc.) and your non-necessities (social life, traveling, savings, etc.). Unless you are blessed with an unlimited amount of income through a trust fund or a lucky lotto pick, you're going to need to take what you learned in college and apply it to the real world. The great news? A 2019 CareerBuilder study revealed that 80 percent of companies plan to hire college graduates. They need you! They have jobs for you! You've just got to find them.

Maybe you're like me, unwilling to wait and see where fate takes you. You're more of a planner who wanted a job lined up by the time you graduated. Perhaps you took advantage of the career centers and job fairs on campus or turned the internship from last summer into a full-time job that was waiting for you upon graduation. If that sounds like you and you already have a job while reading this, that's awesome! You get to pass the next few chapters and jump to the section on managing all of the money that you'll be making. Now, for the rest of you, let's figure out how to put that degree to use and get paid for it!

WHEN DO COMPANIES START LOOKING FOR ENTRY-LEVEL CANDIDATES?

Although it is estimated that 36 percent of hiring managers will have done the majority of their graduate hiring before June, the majority hire in the third and even into the fourth quarter. A hiring study conducted by CareerBuilder.com revealed that the majority of their recruitment will take place in the third quarter (July to September). However, this job offer doesn't just show up. Remember, almost two million people are expected to graduate in 2020 (according to the National Center for Education Statistics), and these fellow graduates have shiny new bachelor's degrees, just like you. They also need jobs, just like you. Most universities offer career centers and career fairs on campus, making it convenient to market yourself and learn about any available openings. But even with connections like this, it's going to take significant effort to land a job, so it's time to get to work!

WHERE CAN YOU FIND AVAILABLE JOBS?

Although there are still jobs advertised in the classified sections of newspapers, most people find their jobs in other ways. Let's start with the updated version of the "classified ads:" online job sites. Websites like indeed.com, monster.com, and careerbuilder.com are packed with job postings. These online resources house thousands of jobs across the entire country (and, in some cases, the world), hitting on all fields and all levels. Similarly, LinkedIn.com is a great place to search for jobs and make yourself available for jobs.

You may have heard the phrase "it's not what you know, it's who you know." Having a great network of people around you

Before we explore why you may benefit from working with recruiters, let's talk about why companies choose to work with external recruiting agencies. Companies pay a premium to work with external recruiters because they're looking to save time during the hiring process. They want to ensure that the candidates they see have been vetted and measured against the open job requirements. Even though they may have an internal human resources team, that team generally has more than one position they're filling, and they're flooded with resumes. Job search site TheLadders.com reports that, on average, hiring managers spend less than ten seconds looking at each resume. *Less than ten seconds.*

One benefit of recruiters is that many are specialized. They may focus on high tech jobs, the financial industry, the creative space, or the medical field. All they do, all day long, is work with candidates doing what you do...or what you hope to do. They have expertise in that area and know what companies are looking for. Hiring managers know this and would prefer to work with someone who "speaks the same language" as they do instead of being dependent on a generalist or an automated process that relies solely on buzzwords they see on a resume.

In January 2020, Glassdoor (one of the world's largest recruiting sites) shared that the average corporate job posted online receives 250 resumes. Two hundred and fifty! Put yourself in the hiring manager's shoes. If you had the option of sifting through those 250 resumes, none of which have been screened, or looking at three or four resumes that have been pre-screened by a recruiter, which would you choose? And which group would you like to be in as a candidate? There's a far better shot that your resume is getting in the hands of a hiring manager through a recruiter than through an online job portal.

Many hiring managers have partnered with staffing agencies for years, and over that time, a natural relationship develops. These firms know what the manager likes and doesn't like and therefore can better screen and prepare candidates for jobs. A good recruiter will put you through a lengthy screening process. Often it involves a phone call, followed by a resume review and additional screening from there. They'll want to talk to references and meet you in person if possible. This may seem like a lot of work from the candidate's perspective, but remember, they are an extension of the hiring process.

The great news is that recruiters represent many companies and many hiring managers, so once you're through this process, you are now marketable to multiple positions. If a recruiter gives you tips to adjust and tweak your resume, take them up on that advice. Be wary of recruiters who ask you to fabricate your work experience; that is a red flag for sure. However, they may ask you to shuffle the order around or add more bullets around a particular skill set or experience you have in order to appear more marketable to a hiring manager. The depth of your experience may currently be summed up on your resume under one bullet point, but perhaps expanding it by a few bullets will lead to an interview. Remember, a recruiter's job is to get you the interview. Once you get the interview, it's your responsibility to take it from there.

RECRUITERS ARE ABLE TO HELP YOU FIND EMPLOYMENT IN THREE WAYS

1. *Direct placement*

The first is via "direct placement." This means that you are introduced to a company by the recruiting firm, but you are hired by the actual company from day one. You are a full-time employee of that company, are paid directly by that company and, in turn, absorb all of the benefits that the company offers to all of its employees. In this case, the recruiting firm is compensated by the end client (that's your new employer). They usually collect the equivalent to 15 to 25 percent of your first year's salary. Because of this, it's in the recruiter's best interest to get you the highest salary possible. Their firm brings in more if you are paid $52,500 instead of $50,000. Having said that, the goal is to get you the job, so if all other candidates are in a salary range of $48,000 to $50,000, it's the recruiter's job to let you know that your salary expectations are too high. If your minimum salary of $52,500 is firm, let the recruiter know—but also be prepared to be passed up for the job if equally qualified candidates are willing to take the job for less money.

2. Contract

Another way to partner with a staffing company is via a contract opportunity. In this case, you are a temporary employee of the staffing company, getting paid hourly but working onsite at the end client's location. Many staffing firms are now offering benefits such as paid time off and medical benefits, so even though you're paid hourly by the staffing company, you may be able to reap the benefits of a full-time employee. The end client pays the staffing company a certain amount per hour for each hour you work, and then the staffing company pays you a direct labor rate per hour.

For example, let's say the end client pays the firm $45/hour; you may only see $25 of that. It may frustrate you to think of a company making a $20 profit off of you each hour; however, it's not that simple, and that's not all profit. There are massive operating costs for these firms, including salaries for internal employees as well as the technology costs to source and house all of the candidates they speak to on a daily basis. There is an incentive for a recruiter to pay you less per hour because they are paid based on the profit the firm makes per hour. Having said that, no one gets paid if you don't get the job. They may want you to consider taking a dollar or two less per hour, and that's because they make more when they confirm you at a lower hourly rate. They also know that if you are feeling underpaid in a role, you'll start looking for a new role and leave their project, which is no good for anyone, especially the recruiter.

Knowing all of this, make sure that you are upfront and honest about what you need and what you want when it comes to an hourly rate. Ask them to share what other candidates who are being considered for the roles are being paid and use that information to make the best decision. Also, assuming you're working forty hours per week, you can do some math and multiply your hourly rate by forty hours to see how much you'll bring home weekly. When you calculate that figure for the entire year, you can have a better understanding of what a comparable salary would be.

Sometimes these contract roles are open-ended and other times they have a definitive end date. Even if you're on a contract for a set amount of time, a client can terminate the contract for any reason with little to no notice. If they aren't satisfied with your work or feel that they don't need as many people as they've hired, they may cut the engagement short. Depending on the state that you live in, you may be entitled to some unemployment or "bench time" until the firm puts you back to work or until you find another role on your own.

3. Contract-to-hire

The third way a firm can engage with candidates is on a contract-to-hire basis. In this case, you're a contractor for a set amount of time, but the intention of the end client is to make you a full-time employee when given the chance. This way, both of you get a chance to "date" each other before deciding if you want to get married. I'll talk more about this on the coming pages, but for now, know that you'll be employed by the staffing company during the "contract" portion of the role and then convert to a full-time employee. This formally ends your engagement with the staffing company and so you're now working directly with the end client itself.

There's no cost to you to work with recruiters. Partnering with a recruiter or two serves as an extra set of eyes on the market on your behalf. Remember, the goals are the same: you want a job, and they want to help you find that job. You are still completely free to look for employment on your own and to work with multiple recruiters until you find something that suits you. Once you start working with a recruiter, there's no commitment to actually accept a role that they help you secure. However, it is important to be honest with them and keep them abreast of your situation on a regular basis. Let them know when you have other interviews and are close to an offer with other companies. Knowing your timeline will help push recruiters to get quicker feedback on any roles that you're in consideration for. And, if you end up finding your job on your own, be sure to let a recruiter know. You never know what may happen in your career down the line. You may need to re-engage with that recruiter for a future role. Gracefully declining a job with a firm is far better than ghosting them, avoiding their calls, or lying to them about what's going on in your world.

FREELANCE VS. FULL-TIME EMPLOYMENT

Freelancers Union (www.freelancersunion.org) represents the almost 57 million independent workers across America. They have almost 500,000 members and serve as a great resource for current freelancers and those who may be considering a career in freelance work in any field. They offer insurance benefits, including term life, disability, liability, health, and dental insurance. Additionally, they offer community, with local freelance hubs in just shy of thirty major cities.

Their recent reports share that one in three Americans—or roughly 42 million people—is considered to be freelance, and there are predictions that freelancers will make up half of the workforce in the coming years.

Many organizations will opt for a "try before you buy" setup before they offer an employee a full-time role. In 2019, 47 percent of companies had plans to hire on a temporary basis to supplement their existing workforce. Sometimes this is due to a short-term staffing gap (due to disability leave or maternity leave), or perhaps they'd rather give prospects a shot to prove themselves on the job. In the latter case, you get an opportunity to get your foot in the door when you otherwise may not have. The company is able to evaluate your performance on the job and see how culturally compatible you are. You can also do the same. Because the thing is that even if the interview goes perfectly, it's hard to truly predict how well an employee will perform in a job and how well the job will fit with the employee's needs. For example, you may be offered a six-month contract-to-hire role. What this means is that you are paid hourly, sometimes by the company itself or sometimes through a third-party staffing company, for the first six months. At the end of that period of time, you will either have your contract extended, be let go, or get offered full-time employment. In some cases, there's an option to convert you to a full-time employee well before the six months. Perhaps the company has the need for a full-time employee but the budget hasn't been approved yet, so they're able to bring you on in an hourly capacity, which may come from a different budget. As soon as the full-time role is approved, they are able to offer it to you. Sometimes the hourly setup is working. Maybe you're getting benefits from the staffing company you're working with. Maybe you are still attached to your parents' benefit plan and you're liking the fact that you're being paid hourly, which is often more than what you'd be making on a salaried basis.

Beyond the financial benefit, working with a variety of teams across a variety of companies allows you to form bonds with people within your industry, which is expanding your network. These relationships can prove to be helpful in the future as you move to different organizations and can rely on these peers for references, introductions to hiring managers at other companies, insight into upcoming networking events, and opportunities to expand your professional network.

Freelancing also offers you a chance to diversify your experience. As a recent graduate, you may be able to spend time in a massive, well-known organization and then take a role at a small, 25-person start up. And while the prestige of working for a big brand name may impress your family at Thanksgiving, you may realize it's not all that it's cracked up to be. You may thrive in a smaller environment. As you go from role to role, you'll be building a resume where you've been exposed to different technologies, work environments, and challenges that will make you more marketable to a future employer.

After reading the section above, the idea of freelancing—and particularly working from home in your pajamas—may seem enticing, but before you commit to a career in freelance work, know that it's not a career for everyone. Consider the following questions, and then decide if it's the right environment for you.

DO YOU WORK WELL ON YOUR OWN, AND COULD YOU FLOURISH WORKING FROM HOME?

If you don't have professional experience under your belt, you may not know this answer. But think about group work from college. Did you enjoy the energy of working with a team, or do you feel more productive on your own? Can you follow deadlines without a boss breathing down your neck, or do you need that accountability from someone in authority? The flexibility can be both a blessing and a curse, and, depending on how you'd respond, you'd have to consider if you'd thrive with the independence that freelancing provides.

DO YOU HAVE A STRONG NETWORK OF CONTACTS?

Many people don't start freelancing right out of college because they don't have a professional network yet. Often they work up to a point where they feel comfortable that their network of contacts will be able to generate enough work to keep them busy at the level they're looking for. In your case, perhaps you start out doing some side work for a few clients in addition to your full-time job. Then, after a while, each of those clients has more work for you, and if you feel that the workload in the pipeline is enough to sustain your current needs and lifestyle, then maybe it's the time to switch from full-time employment to full-time freelancing.

DO YOU HUSTLE?

When no one is looking, are you getting after it? Doing the work? Getting it done no matter what? Remember that as a freelancer, you're your own boss. You're also your own marketing, sales, public relations, and customer service department. You have to be constantly networking and putting yourself out there. You may spend all day, or all week, emailing and pitching people for their business only to hear "no." What's the plan then? Finding a balance between completing the work you have and securing future work will take time.

ARE YOU ORGANIZED?

Without the formal structure of a corporate environment, you'll need to put some systems and processes in place to manage all the projects that are coming in and not let deliverables fall through the cracks. Tracking hours correctly and invoicing the right customers for the right work is critical; otherwise, you'll lose credibility with the very clients you are trying to establish a relationship with. Plus, you want to get paid, right?

WHAT DOES THE CONCEPT OF "JOB SECURITY" MEAN TO YOU?

Many people feel that a full-time job is more secure and, in some ways, it may be. You don't need to be the one worrying about drumming up business, and you know that you're going to collect a paycheck at the end of every two weeks. Hopefully.

Unless the company has to down-size and do layoffs. This isn't to scare you, but the idea of "job security" has shifted a lot since our parents were new to the workforce. It's rare that you'll see someone stay with one company for decades. Whether by choice or out of necessity, working full-time somewhere doesn't automatically guarantee job security. And even though it comes with more responsibility, you may feel safer by freelancing and being in charge of your own livelihood.

PROS OF FREELANCING

Every hour worked is an hour paid, including potential for overtime work

Tax write-offs mean more money in your pocket

Opportunity to work with multiple clients at once

More money per hour when compared to a salary

Flexible schedule during week and opportunity to take off between projects

CONS OF FREELANCING

No paid vacation or employer benefits. You are responsible for your own insurances and expenses.

Lack of stability

Responsible for finding your own work

You may find yourself putting in much more than 40 hours of work in one week as you approach a client deadline

Freelancing full-time may scare you. And that's okay; you may not be ready to take on the risk of making this your only source for income. In that case, more and more people are turning to side freelancing gigs for supplemental income to help with their monthly cash flow and add to their resume. If you're just getting your foot in the door as a graphic designer, you may pick up some small side work to add to your portfolio and make a little extra money each month.

Or you could dabble in a part-time job that is totally unrelated to your full-time job. Maybe you babysit every now and then or partner with TaskRabbit.com to find short-term gigs helping people around their homes. Additionally, more and more people are exploring opportunities within the Multi-Level Marketing (MLM) world due to the flexibility it provides and the upside that's possible. Additionally, investing some of your spare time in obtaining a certification in one of your passions could prove to be helpful down the road should you ever face unemployment or want to supplement your income during various seasons of life.

While I was in college, I knew landing a teaching contract could be challenging. Subbing pays nothing, and I knew I wouldn't be able to support myself and my son until I found a permanent teaching position. I decided to get licensed as an aesthetician and worked as a makeup artist for years at a local salon. I am so thankful that I did! I always had a steady flow of cash from freelancing for weddings, dances, etc. If I wasn't able to sub during the week, at least I could work on the weekends doing make up and making money."

-Julie, Temple University, Class of 2008

THE IMPORTANCE OF YOUR RESUME

Long before you come in for an interview, your resume is seen and scrutinized by several people on the hiring team. A recruiter or member of the Human Resources (HR) team is often the one who decides if your resume reaches the inbox of a hiring manager. Then the hiring manager, and perhaps other members of the team, decides if your resume warrants an interview. Therefore, your resume must provide a great first impression.

When it comes to listing your employment history, don't oversell it. We know high school jobs are just that: jobs they give to high school students. You were a waiter? Great! We've all been to restaurants and many of us (myself included!) have been waiters or waitresses in the past. If you want to include high school and college jobs when crafting your resume, include some key bullets about what you spent your time doing. Although you don't want it to sound overly simplified, spell out, literally, what you did as a server. You took and served orders, refilled soft drinks, hoped to not spill those drinks on customers, and, ideally, collected a tip at the end. You were on your feet, hopefully you didn't mess up too many orders, and you didn't deal with too many assholes. And there you go—your serving career summed up in a few bullets. Highlight if you had any leadership roles (training new hires, filling in as manager when needed, responsible for collecting money from other employees at night), but don't over-promote what you did. No need to waste precious resume space with something like, "Provided exceptional customer service to hundreds of customers who enjoyed the delicacies of Old World Italy. Additionally, I made cuisine recommendations for patrons while simultaneously balancing six to eight drinks on a tray, two of which were martinis." (Author's note: If you order martinis and they don't spill en route to you, tip that server well. If you know it spilled a lot on the voyage from the bar to your table, tip even more. That shit is hard!)

Employers want to see evidence of your work ethic. Holding down a job and a full course load is not an easy feat. Throw in some leadership—not just membership—in extracurricular activities, a decent GPA and a collegiate sport on top of that? I'm impressed. To me, that shows that you have the ability to manage your time well (the busy schedule) and focus on what's important when it's important (sports when you were playing/practicing and academics when you're in class, as evidenced by the GPA). It also illustrates the fact that you didn't just do the bare minimum by attending the occasional meeting of the American Marketing Association; you actually did something to contribute to the organization. It shows a little more initiative than the person lacking that on their resume. Look, most hiring managers also went to college. They drank too much on Thursdays and barely made it to their Friday classes. They also halfway attended meetings just to be able to include it on their resumes. They've been there. They get it.

But what if you didn't work while in high school or college? What if you didn't join the clubs? Since you can't go back in time, how do you illustrate your strengths? In this case, you need to be armed with examples of how your skills have shined in real-life situations. If someone asked you why you were qualified for the job and you had to rattle off a few qualities and reasons why you're their person, what would you say? Take each of those traits you listed (hard-working, dedicated, able to overcome adversity, creative, etc.) and connect them to a time where those qualities were illustrated in your actions. Think about experiences in school and group work. Think about the goals you set and went after in high school, in the classroom or on the field. Think about personal adversity that tested your faith and character, and be proud of being able to live to tell about how you made it through. Not all relevant experience comes from the clubs you were part of or the jobs that you had. You've got more to offer than you think you do; spend some time really thinking about all of this as you start preparing for your job search and subsequent interviews that will follow.

BEST PRACTICES FOR WRITING A GREAT RESUME

There is so much free resume advice out there and, as is the case with information overload, you may find conflicting opinions on the format, length, layout etc. Here are some basics that will likely be common across all sources of information that cover the topic of resumes.

1. **Look:** Aim for consistency. Make sure it's all in the same font—a basic, boring font that's the same size throughout the document and no smaller than 11 pt. Make sure everything is aligned to the left side of the page. If you decide to bold the names of the companies you worked for, cool. Do that with each company. If you decide to italicize the locations of the companies, great. Make sure that's consistent throughout. If you abbreviate the month you started or quit, do that for each entry. If you decide to use numbers to indicate your dates instead, you're welcome to, but (you guessed it) do that every time. When you're printing your resume, make sure you invest in some good paper. Don't use generic printer paper you stole from your school's copy center. Head to Staples and buy a 25/50 pack of higher-quality paper. You can find what you need for $10-$15, and trust me, it's worth it. I would also recommend that you spend a little bit of money and have them printed on a professional printer. Local printing shops or office supply stores can help you with this. I've seen resumes where the ink is slowly running out as the words approached the bottom of the page. Trust me, I've been there, trying to print at home and suddenly realizing you're out of ink. It always happens when you have somewhere to be, right? What that tells me is that you didn't plan ahead, waited until the last minute to print, and didn't have time to stop somewhere else for a "Plan B" option. Will it prevent you from getting the job? Maybe not. But, if I'm reading it as a hiring manager, I'm already concerned about your ability to prioritize tasks and manage time well. Don't

give the interviewer a reason to think anything negative about you before the interview has even started. Take a look at the resume below. See how it doesn't look consistent? Dates are captured in different ways, fonts look like they've been cut and pasted, italics are used randomly, and the spacing looks off. Come on; you can do better than that! Don't let the look of your resume take away from the content of what's on the resume. After all, this is your calling card. Make sure it's the best representation of you.

2. **Length:** I don't see any reason why your resume, for an entry-level job, needs to be more than one page. Going into great detail about the one high-school fundraiser you chaired as a sophomore isn't necessary and doesn't deserve lines and lines of your limited space. Now, if you really want to explain that you have experience chairing a fundraiser, especially if it's relevant for the job you're applying for, then include it. Just note it on your resume and be sure to bring it up when in the interview. Create something as simple as a "Fundraising Experience" header followed by a short list of different events or simply "Volunteer Experience: Big Brothers/Big Sisters, Habitat for Humanity, MS Walk." It doesn't take up much space, the interviewer sees it, and you are reminded to use it as a talking point without stealing precious space from the bulk of your experience. Also, don't include references on the same page as your resume. You could include a line that says "references available upon request" at the bottom or leave it off completely and have a second page ready to hand the interviewer before you leave.

3. **Lies:** *Do not* include any lies. Even if it feels tempting, don't do it. Don't stretch the dates of employment; this will all be validated at some point before you're offered the job. Did you have a break between jobs or not work a semester in college? That's okay. Just be prepared to talk about it. I'm okay with someone saying to me that they had to stop working as a sophomore because they didn't

do as well as they hoped to as a freshman and needed to get their grades up before going back to work. What's even better is if they were able to work as a junior because they figured out how to manage it all. That actually bodes well for a candidate in my book.

Most interviewers admit that they've caught people in lies before and even more candidates have admitted that they've "embellished" their experience. Trust me, this shit will reveal itself further in the interview process or once hired. It's not a good look—ever. You need to be able to back up whatever is on your resume, to whatever level of experience you claim to have. If you start with only the truth on your resume, you'll be able to speak to it correctly while interviewing.

4. **Contact information:** At the very top of your resume, you need to include your mailing address, phone number, and email address. Do your best to squeeze this onto one line if possible.

If you are interviewing for a job in a different geographic area and have a local address within that area, use that. For example, if you currently live in Washington, DC, but are interviewing for a job in NYC and will stay with a family member locally while getting settled, use the NYC address. This is important because when recruiters are searching for candidates, that local zip code will come up in their search. Additionally, if a hiring manager gets a stack of resumes and has to choose from local candidates or out-of-state candidates, often they'll lean toward the local candidates if the resumes are similar. The reason is that a local candidate is perceived as easier to deal with. They are usually able to come in for job interviews faster, they already know about the cost of living and the intricacies of the city where they'd be working, and they may not expect any sort of relocation package. When a hiring manager hears that someone from far away wants to relocate to their town, they may question how serious that candidate is and may opt to move forward with local candidates first. If you're already there, you show a visible commitment to working in that area.

When listing contact information, you'll also want to include your cell phone number. Please record a new, professional-sounding voicemail if the one that you have is more casual. It doesn't need to be anything too stuffy; just make sure that you clearly state your first and last name and that there's not a ton of background noise. Keep in mind that this may be one of the first impressions that a hiring manager has on you. Make sure your voicemail isn't full and that you're able to receive messages. Also, if your voicemail currently says, "You have reached the voicemail of 215-555-1234," change it to include your name. And check your voicemail often. The last thing you want to do is miss an interview request that is waiting for you!

Now, let's talk about your email address. This may be something you're already aware of, but it's important enough to mention formally. My college email address was Girl-PleaseJMU@aol.com. Seriously. Had I included that on my resume, it probably would have raised some questions. I have received resumes with tons of ridiculous email addresses, my favorite being one that started with "xoxocrazychic69" - think I'm eager to bring her (or him?) into my office for an interview? Fair or not, I'm already forming opinions about the person attached to that email address. If you've got an email address like that and you don't want to change it, you don't have to. But for interview/resume purposes, take the time to make a new, more boring, one. Create an email address that includes your first and last name, along with a few numbers if needed. Firstname.Lastname123@whatever.com is a good place to start.

LOOKING FOR "THE PERFECT" JOB

Too often, we're worried about the title on our business card. Someone once shared with me that getting too focused on the title will be distracting. And they were right. Instead, try making a list of "must-haves" for your job. Then think about a list of "nice-to-haves." Finally, think about a list of "deal-breakers"—and go nuts with this list. Add all you want, but be careful how you categorize these items. A must-have means you will not take a job unless it has that item. A deal breaker is something you won't tolerate, for instance, inflexible working hours. If you're offered a job that has all of the items in the must-have column but also one of the deal-breaker items, then forget it. Not the job for you.

> *I was not as serious about the job hunt as I should have been. I was waiting for the "perfect job" - which to me, was getting paid to do something that I was super excited about. After going on a ton of interviews and taking odd jobs (soccer coach, part time at Jamba Juice and babysitting), I found myself running very low on money and had to settle for any job"*
>
> - Natalie, University of California, Berkley, Class of 2001

I didn't have a great list when I first graduated. I only knew I wanted to live in San Diego, and for two reasons. First, have you been? If not, go there, and then you'll know. Second, that's where my boyfriend (now my husband) lived, and I was tired of our long-distance relationship. I took the first job I was offered, which, looking back, was the best training I could have received for my career. At the time, it was unsexy and demanded long hours, including nights and weekends. I was working on commission only and constantly hiring and firing, doing my best to hang on to the right people who came into our company. Like I said, I had no list. But, when I was leaving that job after two years, I decided to take what I loved about the job and leave out what I didn't.

Here's what my list looked like at age twenty-four, as I was figuring out my next move:

MUST HAVES	NICE TO HAVES	DEAL BREAKERS
Opportunity to grow professionally; a path towards management	Light travel as part of the job	Relocation
Commission plus base - had to cover my expenses	Within 20 minutes of my apartment	More than an hour commute each way
Ongoing training	Diverse team	Mandatory weekend and night work
Working with a supportive team	Ability to learn from women in leadership roles	Commission only
Large, reputable company	Ability to work from home occasionally and/or dress casually	
Great corporate culture		
In front of clients/customers building relationships than in front of a computer		

See how general that list is? It's not very specific. It talks a little bit about a career path, mentions salary structure, and hits on the company and culture. Now, think about some of the most well-known companies, the ones that are often featured in case studies for business classes. Let's start with Southwest Airlines; this company probably hits all of the must-haves, but, depending on the role, it also may include some deal-breakers. I may have to work at night or on the weekends. Plus, they are headquartered in Texas, so relocation may be necessary. Even though the company is likely an excellent place to work, a job there may have had two of the three deal-breakers on my list. What about Google? Again, it probably hits most of my must-haves, but it would depend on my role at the company. If I interviewed for a computer engineer role there, I might not be able to be in front of clients and customers, even though I work for a "large and reputable company."

What does your list include? Everyone has their own personal requirements for what they look for in a job, and there are no wrong answers here. Think about what's important to you. Perhaps you refuse to wear anything other than jeans to work. That's cool; you just need to determine if it's a must-have or a nice-to-have. If you find a job that's going to pay well and has a short commute to your house with an opportunity for you to grow, but you need to wear a suit, will you turn it down? If you have jeans as a "must-have," you will. If you have it as a "nice-to-have," you may accept the job and settle for the occasional "jeans Friday" your company allows during the summer months. Make your list your own. It's no one else's. Not being honest with yourself when creating this list may lead to a decision that's not fully aligned to what's important to you.

Once you have a couple of jobs in mind, have a resume that you feel proud of and are ready to go on some interviews, here comes the fun part! Keep reading to learn more about how to prepare for—and crush!—all of the interviews you attend.

Key takeaways:

1. START LOOKING FOR JOBS ONLINE ON SITES LIKE MONSTER.COM AND CAREERBUILDER.COM, AS WELL AS SPECIALIZED SITES UNIQUE TO YOUR FIELD OF STUDY.

2. CONNECT WITH YOUR COLLEGE'S CAREER CENTER TO LEARN WHAT TYPE OF ALUMNI SERVICES THEY OFFER. EVEN THOUGH YOU ARE NO LONGER A STUDENT THERE, THE RESOURCES THEY OFFER COULD PROVE TO BE VERY BENEFICIAL TO YOU.

3. KEEP IN MIND THAT PARTNERING WITH A RECRUITER MAY HELP YOU GET YOUR RESUME IN FRONT OF MORE MANAGERS AND SEPARATE YOU FROM THE REST OF THE 250+ CANDIDATES WHO WILL APPLY FOR THE SAME JOB AS YOU.

4. UNDERSTAND THE DIFFERENCES BETWEEN FREELANCE AND FULL-TIME WORK, AND DO YOUR RESEARCH BEFORE DECIDING WHETHER OR NOT A FREELANCE CAREER MAKES SENSE FOR YOU.

5. MAKE SURE YOUR RESUME IS A PROFESSIONAL REPRESENTATION OF YOU. ENSURE THAT THE FONT AND SPACING IS CONSISTENT THROUGHOUT THE ENTIRE DOCUMENT. MAKE SURE IT'S PRINTED ON RESUME PAPER, AND AIM TO KEEP IT TO ONE PAGE OR LESS. AVOID THE TEMPTATION TO INCLUDE ANY "EXAGGERATIONS" OR OUTRIGHT LIES ON THE RESUME, AND MAKE SURE IT INCLUDES UPDATED AND PROFESSIONAL CONTACT INFORMATION (CHECK THE EMAIL ADDRESS THAT YOU'RE INCLUDING ON THE RESUME AND CHANGE IF NECESSARY).

6. CREATE A LIST OF "MUST-HAVES," "NICE-TO-HAVES," AND "DEAL-BREAKERS" BEFORE APPLYING TO AND INTERVIEWING FOR ANY OPEN POSITIONS. IN FACT, YOU CAN APPLY THIS APPROACH TO MOST DECISIONS IN LIFE INCLUDING HOUSING CHOICES, RELATIONSHIP CHOICES, FUTURE PURCHASES, AND SO ON.

Chapter Four

HOW DO I LAND A GREAT JOB?

You've done all of the research and all of the applying, and congratulations: you have some interview requests! This is your chance to learn more about the open roles and showcase the skills that you have in the hopes that the role is a great fit for you. You've come this far, and now your task is to nail this interview. Even if you're unsure whether or not the role is right for you, preparation is key. As mentioned before, I have a decade and a half of experience interviewing people in various organizations, and boy, do I feel like I've seen it all. Please, if you remember nothing else in this book, please prepare for your interviews.

HOW TO PREPARE FOR THE INTERVIEW

The following are some key tips for performing well in an interview:

1. **Do your research:** Know whom you're interviewing with, details of the job you're interviewing for, and basics on the company that you're hoping to work for. True, you will learn a lot once you're in the interview,

but there is so much free information out there about all three of those areas, and not doing some homework before-hand is a recipe for disaster. Each company's website has an "About Us" section with a layman's term description of what they do and often what they stand for. There are probably press releases floating around out there too. This is information that the company itself puts out there for this exact purpose: they want people to know specific facts about them. If you don't know whom you're interviewing with, you can search the company on LinkedIn and start exploring some of the employees who work there. Reach out to some. Be bold, and let them know that you're interviewing for a role there and that you're wondering if they'd be willing to hop on the phone with you to chat a bit. Maybe you notice that your friend's mom is connected to someone who looks pretty important there. Perhaps she can make a connection on your behalf. You'd be surprised how many people are willing to help if you simply ask. They may decline, but I can promise you that they definitely won't help if they're never asked. As a side note, it is vital that you have a presence on LinkedIn. It's a differentiator between you and other candidates who may not have their resume, accolades, and recommendations visible for a hiring manager to see.

> " I was called by Ritz Carlton while I was working at Hyatt, and I was doing very well so when they 'recruited' me, I was cocky and didn't prepare. Their line of questioning was very specific and about luxury sales; I was 22 and had no concept of luxury. I didn't get the job—or a 2nd interview. Always prepare and do research. Know the company, know the job, have questions prepared for the interviewer."
>
> - Nikki, James Madison University, Class of 2005

2. **Make sure you're able to speak to everything on your resume:** It's all fair game. If you say you're "proficient in Excel," you need to be prepared for them to question you on that. You're fluent in Spanish? Perfecto! You'd better be prepared for the entire interview to be in that language. You said you volunteered at a homeless shelter? Be ready to talk about that experience in detail. Be honest with what you put on your resume, and be honest when you talk about it. If all you know how to say in Spanish is, "Me gusta ir a la biblioteca" (basically all the Spanish I know), then don't say that you're fluent. Me sientes? Oh, don't know what that means? If you knew Spanish, you would (wink wink).

3. **Come prepared with questions:** Have inquiries that are crafted specifically for the interview that you're on. Use what you found in your research to make it less general and more specific, such as, "I noticed on the job description it mentioned an extensive sales training program; could you please walk me through what that entails?" Or, "I see that you were recently voted one of the best places to work; congratulations! In your opinion, why do you think that is?" Do you see the difference between saying that and something like, "Why do you like working here?" When you prepare, you don't sound like a know-it-all; you sound like someone who has done her research. Both questions may yield the same answer, but the way in which you ask it will separate you from the rest of the candidates who are interested in the same role.

4. **Arrive early, and look sharp:** This may seem like a no-brainer, but you'd be surprised by the number of people who arrive in wrinkled clothes, dressed overly casual or looking like they just rolled out of bed; it's alarming. Guys, iron your shirt. If your button-down shirt came folded, please take it out and iron it before the day of the interview. Have your interview shirts laundered by a dry cleaner. It's worth the few dollars per shirt to have them professionally cleaned. I'm all about the facial hair,

but make sure it's cleaned up and under control. Ladies, you don't need to dress like it's your wedding day, but throw some light makeup on, and make sure your hair is styled professionally.

Put some care into your presentation. It's one of the first impressions you'll create with the person interviewing you. Also, dress a little nicer than you think you should. If you're able to find out the dress code before interviewing, take it up a notch. If you know that the company is "jeans friendly," pick a different type of pants for the interview. If you know it's "business casual" and polo shirts are allowed, I'd still recommend a suit jacket or blazer for the interview. You can always take it off. Better to overdress than underdress.

Make sure you know where you're going—confirm the address long before it's time to leave. If you are being extra cautious, take a little test drive to the interview location so you can find the building, suite number, etc. Account for traffic as well. Plan to arrive early, and if you're there more than fifteen minutes early, hang in your car for a bit. Put on your favorite song, review your notes, and then, when it's appropriate, head on in and slay the interview. Now, life happens, I get it. I've had a few people know they were going to be late, and they called ahead of time to let me know. Do I love that they were late? No. But I do appreciate that they acknowledged it and had enough respect for my time to call. If someone was supposed to be there at 2 p.m. and they haven't arrived or called by 2 p.m., I'm upset. What bothers me even more is when they stroll into the lobby at 2:10 as if nothing happened. Did they not think I'd notice that they were late? The interviewer has likely reserved up to an hour to meet with you. Don't disrespect their time by being late, and if you are late, don't disrespect them further by not owning up to it. (FYI, I have hired people who have been late and professionally apologized. I have yet to hire someone who was late and offered a lame apology only after I brought up their tardiness.)

> *One time I was interviewing for an orthodontic residency position in Chicago. I got completely turned around on the way there, took the wrong train connection, and was thirty minutes late. Then, in my interview with the director of the program, I accidentally called her by the wrong name. Needless to say, it didn't go so well."*
>
> - Preston, University of Texas at Austin, Class of 2009

5. **Have a clean notebook and a pen with you:** Ideally, this is not a notebook that has also been used to jot down notes from your past classes. Invest in a nicer portfolio that holds a legal pad. All college bookstores have an overpriced one with your alma mater embossed on the front cover. You can also find more generic ones almost everywhere. Inside, have the questions you plan on asking neatly written down. Please do not have them on your phone. Ask the interviewer if it's okay to write notes throughout the interview. They will always say yes, and you may score a few points by asking that question. An interview is two-way; you should be interviewing the company just as much as the company is interviewing you. If I'm interviewing you and you don't have a notebook, I'm wondering just how serious you are about the role and curious how you will retain all of the information discussed? You can also write down things that stood out while in the interview, and these things can be used later to follow up in your thank-you note (more to come on that later). Also, before leaving, ask for a business card if you haven't already been given one.

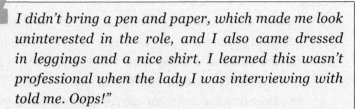

I didn't bring a pen and paper, which made me look uninterested in the role, and I also came dressed in leggings and a nice shirt. I learned this wasn't professional when the lady I was interviewing with told me. Oops!"

- Ashley Clarke, Fairleigh Dickinson, Class of 2014

6. Turn off your cell phone during the interview: I actually recommend having it turned off by the time you hit the lobby. Don't have it on "vibrate," don't have it flash a light when a call or notification comes in. And put it away! Having it out in front of you, even face down, is a distraction during the interview. Keep it in your pocket, leave it in the car, whatever; just don't let me see it. Also, please don't keep your list of questions on your phone or use your phone to take notes during the interview. I get it; we're all slightly addicted to our phones, but even if using it for a work-related purpose, it's not a good look. The only time I'm good with a phone being out during an interview is if I'm discussing setting up a next step in the interview process. If I asked a candidate, "Could you come in next Tuesday morning for another interview," I'm totally okay if the candidate says, "Would you mind if I check the date in my calendar on my phone?" To me, that's completely fine!

One time, my cell phone kept ringing and buzzing during an interview. They were backed up, so I was there longer than expected. The calls coming through were my neurotic mother wondering where I was and how it went. After the third buzz, I pulled the phone out of my bag and turned it all the way off... I think she may have ruined that one for me!"

- Allyson, Muhlenberg College, Class of 2004

7. **No gum:** I'm all about the fresh breath, but spit that gum out or finish the mint before you walk into the lobby.

8. **Be mindful of your interactions the moment you pull up to the building:** You never know whom you'll be parked next to, with whom you're sharing an elevator, or who may be in the stall next to you. The way you present yourself from the moment you walk into the building is critical. Think about what would happen if you were finishing up a personal call while on an elevator only to see that the person who overheard all about your plans to get shitfaced in Vegas next weekend could be your future boss. What would happen if you got upset about someone stealing your parking space in the lot only to bump into that person an hour later as you're touring the office? Err on the side of being friendly and polite to everyone you see from the moment you pull up to the building. Hell, that's not just while you're interviewing. That's a good life lesson!

PRACTICE ANSWERING COMMON INTERVIEW QUESTIONS

When interviewing candidates, my goal is to get to know that person, far beyond their resume, in a short amount of time. In order to do that, I'm a big fan of situational questions, which help me understand who you are, not just what's on your resume. If you tell me you're a hard worker, I'm looking for evidence of that work ethic. If you tell me you excel in a team setting, I want to hear about how you performed in past group environments. Ten of my favorite interview questions to ask are:

1. *Tell me about a time when you received harsh feedback; what was it, and how did you respond? (I'm looking for how you respond to constructive criticism.)*

2. *What's the toughest thing you've ever been through, personally or professionally? How were you able to overcome that adversity? (I'm looking to see how you react when the going gets tough.)*

3. What did you like about your last manager, and what do you wish he/she did differently? (I'm looking to see how you may blend with my management style; try not to bash your last boss here, FYI.)

4. *If you could go back and hit the reset button on anything you've ever done in your life, academically, personally, or professionally, what would you change? (I'm looking to see how aware you are of past decisions, and what your hindsight has taught you.)*

5. *Talk to me about some of your biggest strengths, and give me some examples of when those strengths were illustrated in your actions. (I'm looking to see how your strengths have manifested in past situations.)*

6. *Walk me through your short-term and long-term goals. (I'm looking to see if you've got specific goals and how you're working toward them.)*

7. *Tell me about a time that you worked with someone who had a different work style than yours. (I'm looking to see how you may collaborate with a diverse team.)*

8. *Tell me about a time where you set a big goal for yourself and missed it. (I'm looking to see how you respond to failure or setbacks.)*

9. *While preparing for this interview, what did you learn about this company? (I'm looking to see if you did any research in advance of this interview.)*

10. *Why do you feel you'll be a great fit for this job, and why do you feel this job will be a great fit for you? (I'm looking to see if you have a good understanding of the job and hear your reasons as to why you think you're a match.)*

DON'T JUST BE INTERESTING - BE INTERESTED AS WELL

It's not just about being interesting - be interested as well. Interviews are for the benefit of both of you. The company is trying to assess if you're a good fit for them, and you should be assessing if the company is a good fit for you. Your goal is to understand if this is a good role for you, and because both of you are expected to come to a decision by the end of the interview process, you want to be sure you're asking as many questions as possible to learn as much as you can.

Knowing this, you'll want to come armed with questions that will give you insight into what it's like to work there. Additionally, your goal should be to ask questions that will give you insight into that "must-have/nice-to-have/deal-breaker list" that you created in the last chapter. When you interview, ask questions that will help you determine if your "must-haves" will be met and if your "deal-breakers" would be avoided. Below is a list of questions you can ask that, when answered, can reveal information that will help you decide whether this company or opportunity is one worth considering further.

1. *"What is your favorite part of working here?"*

2. *"What keeps you coming in every day? What has kept you here for (insert the number of years they've been there) years?"*

3. *"Can you tell me a little bit about your culture?"*

4. *"Please describe what a typical day here looks like."*

5. *"Could you talk to me about the training that the company offers?"*

6. *"Is there a career roadmap for someone in my role? Could you please walk me through that?"*

7. *"Who are your role models here, and what do you admire about them?"*

8. *"What's something you didn't know about the company when you started that has pleasantly surprised you?" Followed by, "Is there anything that you wish you knew before starting that you can share with someone in my position?"*

9. *"Based on our conversation today, are there any areas of concern you have and/or any answers you'd like me to elaborate on?"*

10. *"What are the next steps in the interview process?"*

Their answers may hit a couple of bullets on your list. For example, if someone says, "My favorite part about working here is all the support I get from my team and leadership. I can ask questions without feeling silly. They allow me to work from home when I need to take my dog to the vet or wait for a repairman. I've also been promoted two times in the eighteen months that I've been here." In that one response, you got answers to your questions about culture, ability to advance, flexibility, and support from the team. Now, this may be unique to this one person. There is no guarantee that you will be given the same flexibility or support when you join; however, it's promising to see that an employee at the company has earned that flexibility and growth.

THINGS TO PAY ATTENTION TO

1. **Did that person start in an entry-level job?** Compare apples to apples. You can't expect to get the same level of flexibility or compensation as someone who has been with the company for twenty years. Do your best to find someone who is a year or so ahead of you, in the same/similar role as you're interviewing for. They will give you the most realistic view of what your first one to two years will look like.

2. **Keep in mind that not everyone has the same list as you.** Someone might say, "My favorite part about this job is that everyone leaves me alone. I can do my own thing without having to work with a big team and all the drama that comes along with big teams. You get a lot of independence here." Now, it's nice to have a certain level of independence and autonomy. However, if you're looking to work with a team that is energetic, supportive,

and collaborative, this solitary environment may end up being a reason you leave the company a year from now. To really get to the root of how things are within that company, don't ask leading questions. Don't say, "I really want to work with a big team; can I do that here?" Ask a more open-ended question: "Can you tell me about the organizational structure?" And see what they say.

3. **The bigger the company, the more the culture varies from team to team.** Let's go back to Google. I'm sure that individual groups (engineering vs. sales, HR vs. janitorial) all have different cultures. The best companies have consistency among all teams, but just because someone in sales cites the culture as the best part doesn't mean that someone on the PR team would feel the same way. Again, do your best to speak with people who have similar job responsibilities to what you'll be doing if offered the position.

It's also important to be open to new possibilities in fields you may not have expected to be a part of. I didn't grow up dreaming of being a "recruiter" and I *never* thought I'd be in the staffing/recruiting industry. But when I interviewed for my company at twenty-four years old, it hit all of my must-haves, all but one of my nice-to-haves (flexibility in schedule/dress, which eventually happened later in my career), and none of my deal-breakers. Score! Could I have found a job that met all of them in a different industry? Yes. But I found this one and ended up spending twelve years with that company. Had I passed up on that interview or offer because I never thought I'd see "recruiter" on my business card, I would have missed out on a wonderful, fruitful career with an exceptional company.

INTERVIEW FOLLOW-UP

You may already know that it's polite to send a thank-you note after each stage of your interview process. Today, many companies have you meet with multiple team members, and although it will take more time, it's good practice to individually thank each person you meet with. More and more people send these notes via email, and while this is better than nothing, I'm still most impressed when people kick it old school and send a handwritten note. In fact, if I was considering passing on you for a position and then received a handwritten thank-you note, I may reconsider your candidacy. It's not a guarantee that my mind will be changed, but it will at least make me give you a second look before moving forward with other candidates. If you decide that email is your best option, here are some tips:

1. **Send individual emails to each person.** Don't send one bulk email with everyone cc'd on it. That's impersonal and seems like you rushed it. Spend the extra time to personalize each email. Bring up a specific point discussed during the interview. Let them know you heard what they said. For example, if one person mentioned that they loved working at the company because of the training it offered, you could say something like, "Thank you for taking the time to explain, in detail, the great training that (Company Name) has to offer. That gave me a better understanding of what I'd be exposed to should I be selected for this position."

Another thing you can do is, if you felt that you bombed a question or wish you'd answered it differently, use your note to answer the question in a different way. You could say something like, "After meeting with you, I thought more about the question you asked me about why I wanted this job. I wasn't satisfied with how I answered at the time. I'd like to add that (insert additional info here). I look forward to discussing that further if selected for a second-round interview."

Also keep in mind that when multiple people interview someone, it's likely that the group gets together to discuss the interview with each other. It wasn't uncommon for my team to forward me the thank-you notes that were emailed to them. We'd always remark how impressive it was when someone really tailored the email to that specific person's interview versus copying and pasting the same thank-you note to everyone. We could tell they were listening and engaged. Since we often used email to communicate with clients, comments were made about how impressive their writing was, which scored a point in the "yes" column for that person's candidacy. Spend the extra time here; it makes a difference.

2. **Please check your spelling.** If—after I've just spent an hour with you and you have my business card, looked me up on LinkedIn, saw the nameplate on my door, and received an email with details on your interview (all of which have the correct spelling of my name)—you start a thank-you email to me with "Dear Alisha," I'm going to lose my shit. Look, I know my name isn't Bob or Sue or something with a pretty standard spelling, but not spelling it right shows a lack of attention to detail and, frankly, a lack of thoughtfulness. I'm not saying that the fact that I spell my name "A-l-i-c-i-a" is better than "A-l-i-s-h-a"—it's just not how I spell it. Pay attention to that!

Also, make sure you re-read the email you're about to send. Check all grammar and spelling, or if that's not your strong suit, write it out in a Word document first and do a spell check before cutting and pasting into the body of an email. In fact, the last thing I do when sending an email is putting the person's email address in. Too many times, people enter the email address first and then hit the "send" button before doing a final check. Then we're frantically trying to recall that email once we see a mistake, but it's too late.

Making avoidable mistakes when it comes to spelling and grammar causes me to question your attention to detail and think about how this may affect communication with clients if you're hired for my team. Depending on the position, this could be a make-or-break for the role itself. Either way, slow down and take some time to make it great! It's another way to make a great impression on the people that you interviewed with.

3. **Send a fresh email - do not reply to an email chain that you've used already.** Make it stand out and land at the top of the interviewer's inbox. Something simple like "Thank you for your time" or "Yesterday's interview" in the subject line is enough to convey the topic of the email. You can elaborate in the body of the email.

If, for some reason, you forgot to get the email addresses of the people you interviewed with, feel free to call the company's main line and ask the person who answers the phone if he/she could share that info with you. Saying something like, "I was there yesterday interviewing with Bob and Sue but unfortunately didn't get Sue's business card. I'd like to send her a thank-you note but don't have her email address or the correct spelling of her last name. Could you please provide that?" Most people will be happy to help. Another thing you could do is take a guess at their email. If you interviewed with Mary Smith and know that her email address is msmith@ABCcompany.com, then it's logical to think that Steven Jones would have sjones@ABCcompany.com as his email address. It's not foolproof, as that address could belong to Samantha Jones, but it's at least a good place to start.

If you don't have the last name of the person you interviewed with, ask the person at the front desk before leaving. If that doesn't work, then try searching on LinkedIn. Typing in "Natalie" and "ABC Company" on LinkedIn would reveal any "Natalie's" that have a LinkedIn profile. Their picture and/or title should give you the information you are looking for. You can filter this search further by looking for anyone named "Natalie" that works there currently as opposed to a "Natalie" that has worked there in the past.

Now that I've explained how to properly send a thank-you note via email, I do want to reiterate the impact that a handwritten thank-you card can have. If you happen to have personalized stationery, use that. If not, grab some nice thank-you notes in the card section of any grocery or drug store. Something simple and professional will do the trick. And the same rules mentioned above apply: make it personalized, keep it professional, check the spelling and grammar, and make sure the content is relevant to the recipient. The timeliness of this note is important too. If the company is local, drop the notes off in person the next day. If that won't work, drop them in the mail the next morning so the notes are received in no more than a business day or two from the date of the original meeting. It's a great way to keep yourself fresh in the interviewer's mind, especially if the company is continuing to interview other candidates for the role.

As I re-read this section, I think, "Man, these graduates are going to be scared. It's like the world is against them, and it's going to be nearly impossible to land a job." Here's the good news: the person interviewing you WANTS to fill the job. The vacancy of the job is probably adding strain onto the rest of the team, and the time spent interviewing tons of candidates is taking the interviewer and anyone else involved in the interview process away from their day-to-day tasks. Interviewing loads of people isn't fun—I can promise you that—so the hope is that we find someone who is a slam-dunk, or at least has the potential to be. My goal with this chapter is to arm you with a behind-the-scenes look at what the interviewer is thinking, as well as show you what to avoid and what to pay special attention to in order to better prepare you for securing the right job for you.

Finally, if you don't get the job, I hope you have the courage to ask for interview feedback. I was always impressed by the people who did this either in real time, while in the interview with me, or afterward, when I told them that they didn't get the job. Chances are, if you aren't hired for the job, it's just not the right job for you. The goal of the person doing the hiring is to find the right candidate for the job. And although it may not feel like it if you are still searching for a job, it's better to not be in a job that isn't the right fit for you. Use that interview feedback to better prepare you for the next job.

And if you think, after the feedback you receive, that you want to make one last push to change their mind, give it a shot! It can't hurt. Either you still don't have the job or maybe you get the job after all.

> *I had my first interview with a company I really wanted to work for at a college campus. I crushed it and they wanted to bring me back for a second interview. I assumed they would be paying for my airfare to travel 500 miles for this interview and when I called to inquire about reimbursement, they informed me it was completely up to me. Because this was the only job I wanted, I decided to attend my second interview on the heels of my senior year college spring break. I wouldn't recommend this idea because coming off a 7-day bender doesn't exactly put your mindset in the right place. Needless to say, the second interview didn't go as planned and I never got the call back for a third or to discuss a job offer. I wallowed for about a week, reluctantly accepting a telemarketing job to make ends meet and then had an epiphany. I had been interviewing for a sales role. If I wanted that job badly enough, I had to show that I was willing to do whatever it took to show them I was the right person for the role. Every day for 3 months, I would walk out to a payphone on my 15-minute lunch break and call the office asking to speak with the director of the office. When the receptionist said that she wasn't available, I would ask them to page her. When they told me that she still wasn't available, I left a voice message. This repeated Monday-Friday for 10 weeks until one day she picked up the phone and said, "If you are this persistent about a job, you will be this persistent in what we sell. We still have some questions about you, but let's set some time for one last conversation so we can make a decision." Twelve years later, I retired from that company with over a million dollars in stock. If your gut tells you that the role you want is yours, then go after it as if your life depends on it."*
>
> - Tracy, Florida State University, Class of 1996

HOW DO YOU KNOW YOU'RE BEING PAID FAIRLY?

It's important to know what you're worth, whether you are searching for your first job or you have years of experience. The more information you have, the easier it will be to negotiate your salary. I think we can all agree that the average college student isn't rolling in dough. I can remember many late nights scrounging for quarters—often those set aside to do my laundry—to pay the delivery guy for the very unnecessary (but at the same time totally necessary) pizza.

Once we graduate, we're excited to get a real paycheck, one that will allow us to do all of those things that we couldn't do while in school. Much of my post-college career has required me to interview recent college graduates, and I was continually surprised by the unreasonable expectations that those candidates had. They expected to immediately earn between $60,000 and $100,000 annually, and some of those respondents barely made it through their general education classes. They had no specialized education or training, just a 2.5 GPA in a Liberal Arts education. Although you may come across a job that will have a commission structure where $100,000 in your first year out of school is possible, chances are you're not going to make six figures right out of school. Depending on your major, some entry-level jobs may pay north of $75,000, but it's important to know an appropriate range to shoot for. Know what's reasonable for a graduate with your background so that you can manage your expectations appropriately. This will help you make educated decisions when it comes time to negotiating a salary and ultimately accepting a job.

Your first job out of college is often referred to as an "entry-level" job. This means that you're not in the CEO job, the VP job, the job that gets the flexible schedule, the job that pays six figures, or the job that allows you to do what you want and work how you want. It means that you are likely doing grunt work, reporting to someone who we can only hope is decent and gives you the perfect balance of guidance and autonomy. That's ideal, but often, once you get past the interview and get the offer, you may be disappointed that the job isn't as glamorous as you had hoped. Your goal to work in the fashion industry seemed a lot sexier than what you're actually doing for eight to twelve hours a day. Oh, no one told you? Nine-to-five hours are a thing of the past. Right or wrong, the length of the average workday has changed, and even once you leave the office, you're now reachable outside of working hours due to email, cell phones, and other virtual access to coworkers.

In the summer of 2018, LendEDU, a website that helps consumers learn about and compare financial products, including student loans, personal loans, and credit cards, conducted a survey of 1,000 recent graduates to learn more about what the Class of 2018 was looking for when it came to their careers. Out of the graduates who had secured a job, 33.41 percent were hired at a base salary of $35,000 or lower, and 36.63 percent are making between $36,000 and $50,000. The rest of the respondents made north of $51,000 or preferred not to answer.

DO YOU NEGOTIATE THE SALARY THAT YOU'RE OFFERED?

What happens if the company that you want to work for offers you a position, but the salary comes in a little less than you were hoping for? Do you just say, "I accept" and be thankful that you have a job, or do you press your luck and negotiate a bit? This is a tricky situation, especially for a recent graduate who doesn't have a resume full of professional experience to use as ammunition for a higher salary.

First, take a look at the job you've been offered. If it's a very structured job, such as a military job or one with a government agency, it's unlikely that there's wiggle room. Asking for more will likely be unsuccessful. Also, if a salary range was discussed upfront and you verbally agreed that it was a range you were comfortable with, asking for more once there's an offer may not go over well. If you've been offered a sales job where the base is set but a commission structure is part of your compensation, you can make more money by having a lot of success in the role.

Asking for more of a base salary when there's an upside based on commission is unlikely, especially with no professional sales experience under your belt.

> *My first job was 100% commission. No one to negotiate with but yourself. Great learning experience. Instead of going to grad school, I treated the 5 years I spent in that job as 'Sales Grad School' given the amazing lessons I learned being in the field and experiencing it all first hand. It's the best thing I'd never want to do again."*
>
> - Mike, University of San Diego, Class of 2004

At the time of this writing, it's an employers' market. According to the Economic Policy Institute, the unemployment rate among 2019 college grads is close to 4 percent, which isn't as concerning as the amount of graduates who are underemployed. Underemployment is defined as "working in a job that typically does not require a bachelor's degree." A February 2019 study from Statista, a leading provider of market and consumer data, broke down the amount of underemployment, per major, of recent college graduates between the ages of 22 and 27. A link to the full study can be found in the appendix of this book, but some things to point out are as follows:

* Overall, 42.9 percent of college graduates from all majors were underemployed.

* The major with the lowest amount of underemployed graduates was Nursing, with only 11.4 percent underemployed.

* The major with the most amount of underemployment was Criminal Justice, with 73.2 percent of recent graduates in jobs that do not require a college degree.

* Other majors that reported a 50 percent or more underemployment rate include popular majors such

as Business Management, Liberal Arts, Leisure and
Hospitality, and Marketing and Communications.

I share these figures with you not to scare you but instead
to educate you. It's important to be aware of what's happening
in your particular field of study or geographic area before
deciding whether or not you want to ask for more money. If
you do negotiate, make sure you have a strong case as to why
it makes sense for the company to give you more money. The
majority of the negotiating should be done before you even
enter the conversation with your potential boss. Make sure you
know the general range or standard salary for your role. Utilize
tools like payscale.com, glassdoor.com, and salary.com to help
with this research. Like any resource of a similar nature, these
offer a general range and don't take into account other non-
salary perks that may come along with your job, such as paid
time off, internal stock, bonuses, etc. Be sure to understand the
hiring manager or company's top challenges and be ready to
explain how you can help solve the hiring manager's problems.
Approaching the negotiation conversation in a collaborative
way may yield better results, especially if you keep in mind what
the "other side" wants. If you know someone in your personal
or professional network who has worked for that company, get
some insight on how they have responded to negotiating in
the past and how the company handles raises and promotions.
As a new graduate, you may not have much leverage with the
actual salary, but perhaps you could look at other factors such
as regular face time with a senior leader in the office, flexible
hours, or reimbursement for continuing education or training
that will add to your resume.

Another way to help increase your base salary is by letting
the company know that you have other offers in play. I'm sure
many people bluff here, but I'd recommend only saying that
you have other offers in hand if you truly do. Many times, the
industries are small, and if you say that you have an offer with
XYZ Company, the hiring manager at ABC Company may know
the hiring manager at XYZ. If it's discovered that you were not

honest about having an offer, chances are the initial offer may be pulled back due to dishonesty. If you do have other offers or other pending interviews, you could say something like, "You are my top choice, and I want to be transparent with you. I have two other offers and am expecting a third. If we can get this salary to a number that's fair for both of us, I'm willing to decline those other offers and cancel all pending interviews."

AND IF THEY SAY NO?

If they say no, then the ball is in your court. Are you willing to accept their original offer, or do you need to walk away? If you decide to walk away and cite salary as a reason for declining the job, perhaps they'll bump up that original offer to encourage you to accept the job. But that's not guaranteed. They may have three or four other candidates who are equally qualified for the job and simply move on to the next.

Look at how many irons you have in the fire, how many interviews you have scheduled, and how long you've been looking, and then decide if it's worth the risk. If you're just starting out and have a calendar packed full of interviews, then why not try it? If it backfires you have other opportunities lined up to explore. But the longer you've been looking, the more your tolerance for risk could decrease, and you may accept the job in front of you and hope that your performance on the job will eventually lead to an increase in your compensation. If, over time, you feel like you're being underpaid and don't see it getting better in the near future, you need to decide whether to stick it out or if it's time to start looking for a new job.

DECIDING WHETHER TO STAY OR GO

Remember that list you made before? The one with all the nice-to-haves and must-haves? The one you used to ultimately accept the job you're in? Keep that handy and reference it often. If you're having a bad day, check your "must-haves" and see if they're still being met. Do you still feel like the culture is solid?

Are you still getting the support that you want and need? If those "must-haves" are still available, then know that you're just having a bad day. It's not a reason to leave. On the other hand, if all of a sudden things shifted and your deal-breakers become part of the job—for example, you are being forced to relocate, the compensation structure becomes commission only, or you now have to work each Saturday—well, then, you have a decision to make. Is this something that is still a deal-breaker for you? If so, then it may be time to look outside of your company, or for a different role within your organization that doesn't include those deal-breakers. Also, realize that sometimes your "must-haves" may actually become "nice-to-haves," and a "nice-to-have" may become a deal-breaker or must-have as your personal situation changes. Personally, as my life outside of work evolved (getting married, having children, etc.), the roles I was in still matched up to my "list;" that's why I was able to stay there so long. At the end, that list got out of alignment, and my increased desire for flexibility and entrepreneurship led to my decision to leave. Had I left earlier, during tough seasons in my career, I would have missed out on some of my most rewarding professional years.

Too often, new employees throw in the towel too early. Six months in, you think, "Yeah, this isn't really the job for me." What about it isn't the right fit? What changed? If it's the job you signed up for, and it meets the list you created before, then suck it up and stick it out. The grass isn't necessarily greener somewhere else; it's green where you water it. If your current company is giving you what you need to make your grass green, meeting your must-haves and being mindful of your deal-breakers, then stick it out. Otherwise, you'll end up with two to three jobs on your resume when you're 24. As someone who spent most of her career hiring people in their early 20s, I can tell you that's a turn-off to future employers. I start to wonder what the common denominator is (spoiler alert: it's likely you) and may assume that if you joined my team, things wouldn't be any different. Chances are, you'll be looking for a new job six months after working for me. And that's not a good impression to give off in an interview. Staying at a job for 18 months is an appropriate amount of time to accurately assess whether or not the job is going to be one that you're in for the long haul. At that point, you've got enough personal experience to determine if this is the right role/company/career for you.

"Passion" is often an overused term when describing one's job. Think beyond the specific tasks you're performing daily. Think about how you feel when you leave the office. Think about how you feel while you're there interacting with the teams you work with. Think about how the work you do impacts others. Think about what you're able to do with the money that you're making there. Think about the training you're receiving and the growth you're experiencing while there. That's the stuff I get passionate about, not the fact that I have to attend meetings that often suck or spend my time filling out Excel reports. Who gets excited about that, anyway?

Often I hear something like, "I'm just not passionate about this job." Well, are you passionate about not living with your parents forever? Are you passionate about being able to buy food and pay for WiFi? You can't always get paid for your passions, but that doesn't mean that you have to cut them out of your life completely. Passionate about animals? It doesn't mean you need to become a vet. In fact, sometimes when you marry your passion and your paycheck, you become less excited about the passion in the end. Why not volunteer at an animal shelter a few times a week to fill your "animal-loving" cup? What about fostering dogs for a few weeks at a time? Do you really like music? Awesome! That doesn't mean you need to work for a record label. Perhaps you make a list of all the cool venues in your city and make a goal to see one show at each of them. Or save up some money and travel to see your favorite artist in a new city. Again, just because you don't tie your employment to a passion point doesn't mean you have to have a life without "passion."

If you are passionate about "helping others," you could be a nurse, teacher, pilot, recruiter, or even a school crossing guard. All of these jobs help others in some way but are very different careers. If you want to be "creative," you could be an artist or musician or designer, but plenty of other careers involve some level of creativity. Don't box yourself in by what your job title says or what industry you're in. Happiness in your job and having a meaningful connection to your work transcends industry; you'll find people who love (and hate) their jobs in all industries, at all levels.

Again, the grass is not necessarily greener somewhere else; it's green where you water it. And if you're receiving the seeds, the soil, the sunlight, and the help growing that grass, take a second to do a gut check. You've got to be the one to water it. Are you?

Key takeaways:

1. PREPARE FOR YOUR INTERVIEWS. DO RESEARCH ON THE COMPANY AND THE PEOPLE YOU'RE INTERVIEWING WITH. KNOW YOUR RESUME INSIDE AND OUT. ARRIVE EARLY AND BE PROFESSIONALLY DRESSED. COME ARMED WITH A NOTEBOOK, PEN, AND LIST OF QUESTIONS. TOSS THE GUM BEFORE YOU ARRIVE, AND MAKE SURE YOUR PHONE IS TURNED OFF.

2. PRACTICE ANSWERING COMMONLY ASKED INTERVIEW QUESTIONS, AND USE EXAMPLES FROM YOUR RESUME TO BACK UP ANY ANSWERS YOU GIVE.

3. SEND HANDWRITTEN THANK-YOU NOTES TO EACH PERSON YOU MEET WITH AT EACH STAGE OF THE INTERVIEW PROCESS. IF YOU MUST DO EMAIL, ENSURE THAT EACH PERSON GETS THEIR OWN PERSONALIZED NOTE (INSTEAD OF BEING COPIED ON A BULK EMAIL), AND BE SURE TO RUN A SPELL CHECK BEFORE HITTING SEND.

4. IF YOU ARE NOT SELECTED FOR A JOB, SEEK FEEDBACK TO UNDERSTAND WHY. USE THAT FEEDBACK TO BETTER PREPARE FOR FUTURE INTERVIEWS.

5. UNDERSTAND WHAT A TYPICAL SALARY RANGE IS FOR A JOB SIMILAR TO THE ONE YOU'RE APPLYING FOR. IF YOU ARE OFFERED A SALARY THAT DOESN'T MEET YOUR EXPECTATIONS, DECIDE IF YOU WANT TO ENTER A NEGOTIATION SITUATION WITH YOUR POTENTIAL FUTURE EMPLOYER.

6. KNOW THAT THE GRASS ISN'T ALWAYS GREENER SOMEWHERE ELSE. KEEP REFERRING TO THE REASONS YOU TOOK THE JOB IN THE FIRST PLACE, AND IF, AFTER TIME—IDEALLY A YEAR OR LONGER—YOU'VE REALIZED THAT THE JOB, OR YOUR NEEDS, HAVE CHANGED, THEN IT MAY BE TIME TO START LOOKING FOR A NEW ROLE.

Chapter Five

HOW DO I GET AROUND?

Outside of rent, one of the larger monthly expenses that you may incur after graduation is the cost of transportation. Based on your personal situation, "transportation" may not be limited to a car (and all things related to owning a car, like insurance, gas, maintenance, repairs, tolls, etc.). For some, "transportation" may also be the cost of public transportation, rideshare costs, rental cars, and taxis/car services.

However, most of the chapter ahead will focus on how you navigate the car-buying process. We'll discuss what type of car makes the most sense for you (new or used) and whether buying or leasing makes the most sense for you. But before we talk about how you go about purchasing a car, let's first determine if you even need one.

Here are some things to consider:

WHERE ARE YOU LIVING?

If you're in a suburb, having reliable transportation is key. The further away from a city you are, the less likely it is that you'll be able to rely on any form of public transportation. Sure, there are buses and trains available in some suburban areas, but they tend to run less frequently, which may be a challenge as you plan out your commutes to and from the office.

However, if you live in a major city with a fantastic public transportation system, a car may not be necessary at all. In fact, having a car in a major city is sometimes more of a hassle than a benefit. When you consider the monthly cost to own, maintain, insure, fuel, and park the car, plus any tickets that you may have accidentally collected, a car might not make sense for you. You may be better off taking public transportation to and from work, getting an Uber/Lyft as needed, and then renting a car if you're looking to escape the city on the weekends.

According to the New York City Parking Authority, it currently costs an average of $430/month to park a car in Manhattan. An unlimited subway and bus pass costs $127. When I lived there, it didn't make financial sense for me to own a car. Even when I factored in all the times I took cabs because I was too lazy to walk or didn't want to brave the shitty weather, it was still cheaper than owning a car. Each year, more and more options for rideshares and rental options become available. Hell, you can even scoot your way across some cities on a Bird now! It's also a fun people-watching activity. Watching drunk people try to navigate the scooter is entertaining and concerning at the same time. Check out a local non-profit that focuses on transportation options and see what resources your city has available.

I didn't have a car for the first five years after graduation. I lived in NYC and walked to work while taking taxis and subways on the weekend. The freedom of city life with no car is wonderful!"

- Mary-Paige, James Madison University, Class of 2004

> My husband and I had one car for at least the first five to six years of our marriage. Owning a car is expensive, and there are multiple ways to get around without one. If you live in a place where public transportation is good or walking/biking is an option, do it! It will save you SO much money, and you can always rent a car for road trips or Uber/ Lyft for other events."
>
> – Tricia, Boston University, Class of 1998

> No car, because I live and work in the city. I actually walk to work! I sold my car when I moved into the city for some extra money to start out with."
>
> – Erika, Pennsylvania State University, Class of 2014

WHAT IS YOUR WORK SITUATION?

Do you need to report to an office daily? If so, how far is your office from where you live? Do you have to use my car during the workday to travel to meetings/client sites? Some offices come with ample parking. Other offices require parking permits, and some may not include parking at all. Often, in urban areas, you need to find—and pay for—your own parking. Knowing the cost of this will be important. Perhaps you only work in the office one day a week and the rest of the time you're working from home. If that's the case, you may not need to invest in a new car. The used car that you've owned for years may suffice for the minimal driving you'll be doing.

However, your job may require you to use your car to travel throughout the day to meet up with clients or potential customers. In this case, your car is like an extension of your desk. It plays into your overall professional image, and in many cases, your company may include some sort of car payment or stipend if they're asking you to use your vehicle for work-related purposes. My first company included a car payment in my compensation, but only if I owned a car on their approved car list. Luckily, I was in the market for a new car when I was promoted into this role, so I narrowed my search down to the vehicles that were included on this list. Some of my co-workers weren't as lucky and were forced to sell a car before they were ready because they prematurely purchased a car before securing the job and would have incurred multiple car payments if they didn't part ways with the non-approved option. Whether or not your company is providing any sort of financial assistance for your vehicle, it's important to know how much you'll be driving your car throughout the day. A car with good gas mileage is always nice, but it becomes especially helpful if you're driving more than the average person.

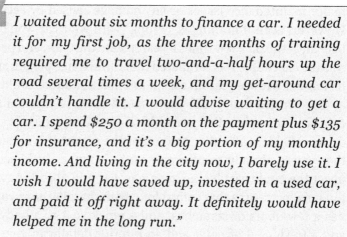

I waited about six months to finance a car. I needed it for my first job, as the three months of training required me to travel two-and-a-half hours up the road several times a week, and my get-around car couldn't handle it. I would advise waiting to get a car. I spend $250 a month on the payment plus $135 for insurance, and it's a big portion of my monthly income. And living in the city now, I barely use it. I wish I would have saved up, invested in a used car, and paid it off right away. It definitely would have helped me in the long run."

– Gianna, Montclair State University, Class of 2015

DO YOU HAVE A CAR NOW?

Is it safe to drive, and does it function well enough to get you from here to there? Do you have a car payment on that car, or has it been paid off? What does your insurance cost each month? What do you like/dislike about your car right now? Can the things that you dislike be improved upon? Ask yourself: why do you want to buy a new car? If you currently have a car payment, make a note of that number. Then add in how much you spend monthly on gas. If you're unsure of this number, take a look at a recent credit card statement and tally up all relevant expenses. What is your monthly insurance payment? Additionally, factor in the number of times you take a cab, Uber, or Lyft each month. Now take that number and multiply it by twelve to find out what you are roughly spending on your car per year. I hope you don't have to deal with any major maintenance issues or any damage caused by accidents. However, even if nothing is "wrong" with your car, you'll need to change the oil a few times a year, rotate the tires, and perform routine checkups. It is estimated that the average person spends just under $1000/year on car maintenance, and it should come as no surprise that you'll likely spend more to maintain your car if it's more than five years old. If your current car is safe to drive, reliable, and either paid off or the payment is an amount that you're already comfortable with, it makes little sense to upset the apple cart by buying a new car and absorbing all the financial pressures that come along with that. Perhaps your car has a few dents or scratches, and a quick visit to a body shop and a fresh coat of paint and an interior detail can give it the facelift you're looking for. Maybe you really want leather seats or a more reliable air conditioning system installed? Those are all after-market additions that can be added to your current vehicle. Yes, they will cost money, but perhaps those additions will grant you some additional time in a car that you've been using for years.

I bought my first car used while I was in college. I kept that car until about four years ago. It wasn't 'fancy;' in fact, it was about as low-budget as you could get. But it worked well, gave me no trouble, and saved me from needing to get a car loan. My husband's mother got him his car as a twenty-first birthday present, and we didn't sell it until he was twenty-nine. That's when we bought our first car together. We didn't trade in my car until our other car was paid off. By doing this, we've managed to keep car debt to just one car at a time. And we definitely go in with a budget and stick to it. I had to pass on the 'better' car because it was going to be $50 more than we were willing to spend. Those little extras add up really fast."

- Colleen, Pennsylvania State University, Class of 2004

My parents and I paid cash for a cheap (but very reliable) Toyota when I was in high school. I drove that car 250,000 miles and never had one issue. I kept that car until just six months ago. My advice is do not buy a car unless you absolutely need to! Not having a car payment is wonderful. A car is not an asset; it's a liability that depreciates the minute you take it off the lot. If you need to buy a car, try to buy used and pay in cash."

- Taylor, University of Kansas, Class of 2015

CAN YOU AFFORD TO ADD A MONTHLY CAR PAYMENT TO YOUR BUDGET RIGHT NOW?

Everyone's situation is unique, and even if you have a car currently, the financial responsibility attached to cars can vary. Maybe it's been paid off already and you are just responsible for the gas, insurance, and upkeep. Maybe your parents are still taking care of your insurance payments and you're making the final few car payments. Perhaps you're in a car that is costing you a ton of money each month and you'd actually save some money by trading it in and choosing a more economical option.

> *I had a car that my grandparents had purchased for me while I was in college, so I didn't have any car payments, but then it kicked the bucket six months after graduation. I ended up buying an older used car. While it was cheap, it "nickeled and dimed" me with repairs, and my rate for the loan was ridiculous. I didn't shop around and just took the first one offered through the dealership."*
>
> – Kendra, James Madison University, Class of 2005

Regardless of your circumstances, it's important to do some math, crunch some numbers, and understand the cost of keeping your car and how that relates to buying a different vehicle at this point in your life. It's important to note that a car is an expensive investment. And when I say investment, I use that term lightly. This "investment" will 100 percent NOT give you a return. The value of a car diminishes the minute you drive it off of the lot. And after that new car smell fades, you're still stuck with the cost of owning a new car.

The problem with the questions I just asked you to think about is that there are some questions you may not know the answer to. Let's say you need to buy a car before you know where you'll be working. Or let's say that you are living at your parents' house for now but don't plan on that being the case for the long run. Perhaps you need a car for a few months, but you plan on moving into the city after you secure a job there. It's a case of "chicken or egg:" you need a car to secure the job, but securing the job first may help you decide whether or not you need to buy a new or used car. You may need to make some assumptions as you work through these scenarios, but do your best to predict the future based on what you know today.

If, after all of the above considerations have been taken into account, you have decided that it's time to swap your current car for a different vehicle (or buy one in the first place), the next step is to figure out how to acquire one. You've got the following options available:

1. Buy/lease a new one
2. Buy a used one
3. Steal one

Technically they're all viable options. But we've got to start narrowing down this list. Let's assume your goal is to stay out of jail; if so, we'll scratch the third option off of the list.

In full disclosure, I don't assign a lot of value to a car. I'm not a "car person" and fully realize that some of you reading this may apply that title to yourself. You may decide to cut costs elsewhere. Personally, I'm not eating ramen and PB&Js daily in order to drive the latest model of an imported sports car. But if you want to splurge on the car of your dreams, you do you, boo. Just ensure that it's accounted for in your monthly budget, and if you can swing it, more power to ya!

You may now be wondering, should you buy new or used?

WHAT ARE THE POSITIVES OF BUYING NEW?

The first—and most obvious—positive of buying a new car is that it's (wait for it...) NEW. There is likely a warranty included in the purchase price that covers (most) anything that goes wrong within a certain number of miles or a specific length of time. You don't need to worry about how the previous owner handled the car, how regularly it was serviced, and what actually went down in that back seat. You are the first one to own that particular car! You may also get a year or so of roadside assistance, which will be appreciated if something happens with the car while you're driving it. In addition to any roadside assistance that comes with the car, consider looking into a AAA membership. It's less than $100 per year, and if you take advantage of the discounts, your card pays for itself even if you never find yourself stranded on the side of the road in need of a tow or staring at your keys inside of your locked car. Many retail stores and most hotels have a "AAA rate;" you just need to show your membership card as proof of an active membership. Gap/Old Navy/Banana Republic will knock 10 percent off of your purchase, and many hotel chains offer $10/$20 off each night of a hotel stay.

Another positive of the new car option is that you'll often get the best financing programs offering little or no interest, which may make the monthly payment on a new car the same or less than a used car. You're also likely to get a car with the highest fuel efficiency standards and all of the latest safety features.

WHAT'S THE DOWNSIDE TO BUYING NEW?

A new car is only "new" while it's at the dealership. The second it is driven off the lot, it begins depreciating. Since you pay a retail price from the dealer, once purchased, it's already dropped to wholesale price. This is the price that a dealer would pay you if you turned around and tried to sell it back to them in a week. While some models handle depreciation better than others, most new car owners can expect that car to lose up to 50 percent of its value within the first three years of ownership. Because they often cost more and they lose value quicker, it's no surprise that buying a new car is a more expensive option than buying used. Additionally, the "new car" label will allow insurance companies to charge you more for your monthly premiums because the replacement costs of a new car, should you need a replacement, are higher than a used car. The final negative to buying new is the first "ding" hurts more than on a used car. Inevitably, you will get a scratch on the outside or a stain on the inside. And when that happens, you're still responsible for the monthly payments.

WHAT ARE THE ADVANTAGES OF BUYING A USED CAR?

We've already hit on the fact that new cars depreciate. Knowing this, buying a car that is at least three years old will save you money when compared to buying the current year's version of that same model. This means you can get more car for your money. Perhaps your current budget will only get you a base model of a brand-new car, but you may be able to get a used but upgraded model of the same car or a different car altogether for the same price or less. Most dealerships offer some sort of "Certified Pre-Owned" (CPO) option, which makes a used-car purchase much less worrisome. All CPO programs vary between manufacturers and dealers, but many come with some level of warranty and additional perks like roadside assistance or loaners when your car inevitably is in need of repair. Because the cost to replace the car—should you be involved in an accident—is less, insurance prices will also be less than buying a new car. Additionally, depending on the state you live in, you may see cheaper registration prices as well.

If you're not buying a used car at a dealership, there are plenty of online resources out there to help you collect data on used-car pricing so that you can be informed when making a decision. Check out CarGurus.com and KellyBlueBook.com to help with this. Make sure you also check out CARFAX.com and AutoCheck.com to look up the history of the used car that you're interested in before you officially purchase it. These reports will cost you a bit, but they can save you money in the long run. VehicleHistory.com is a similar site, but it offers free Vehicle Identification Number (VIN) reports. These reports can tell you what has happened in a vehicle's past and includes information on who owned the car, what work they had done on the vehicle as well as any accidents involving the car. This is critical to know because, although the car may look nice on the outside, you want to know what it's been through to ensure that any damage has been appropriately repaired and no hidden issues exist.

AND THE DOWNSIDE OF BUYING USED?

First, your selection isn't going to be as vast. You have less control when it comes to colors, styles, and options. It comes down to what's available at the time that you need it. If you have some time to search for the perfect used car, you may be able to get more options when it comes to all the bells and whistles, but for many, you'll have to settle at some point and choose the best one up for grabs.

When I bought my car, I knew I wanted a dark blue Nissan Murano with leather seats. That combo wasn't available at any of the dealerships I was working with, so I ended up going with the navy blue model and then installed leather seats after the fact. The other option available was a red version with a fancy screen and built-in navigation system already installed. It was nice, but ultimately it wasn't the color I wanted. It also would have added a considerable amount to my monthly payment. I had to make a choice, and after all, who needs a navigation system anymore— we all use Google Maps or Waze anyway, right?

The other major downside is that it's, as its name says, a *used* car. It has been used... by someone else. And even with a vehicle history report or a certification from a dealership, there's no way to really know how that car was driven or what went on inside that car when it belonged to the previous owner. There's a chance it may be a lemon, and unless you have purchased a late-model used car with some of the original warranty left, you may be on the hook when the first major repair is needed. It's critical to get any used car thoroughly inspected by a mechanic before agreeing to any purchase. It may cost you $100 to have this done, but if you are serious about the car, the $100 is worth it. If you discover that you were about to buy a car in need of significant future repairs, that $100 will have saved you considerable cash down the line. Even if the dealer or seller gives you their word that all is okay, take some time and have a professional— ideally, someone who specializes in the brand of the car you are considering—take a look at the vehicle ahead of time.

If you do need a car, then I would recommend buying a used car that's still in fair condition. You will have plenty of time later in life to have nice material items if you want, but while in your 20s, I think it's great to keep your monthly expenses low so there is money available for experiences (vacations, concerts, things with friends, etc.)."

- Preston, University of Texas at Austin, Class of 2009

> *I bought used cars and all but once had the money to pay for it upfront. There was one time that I bought used and had to make payments but was able to come up with a plan to help me pay if off twenty-eight months earlier than expected and save over $1,000 in interest. If you read financial books on cars, almost all gurus will tell you not to buy new. It always made sense to me not to buy new, at least not until I'm financially free (no student loan debt). I would rather my monthly payments go into paying down my existing debt."*
>
> — Brilynn, NYIT, Class of 2009

Finally, there may be a bit of jealousy that comes with deciding to buy a used car over a new one. You will likely notice cars on the road that are nicer and shinier, while you are stuck with the one that you can afford. For some, this may get under your skin. Others may not mind, or at least will pretend not to mind. Again, I don't consider myself a car person, but if money were no object and I was given the choice of driving a new or used car, clearly I would pick the new car. I think it's safe to say most of us would.

> *I would say don't try to be a hotshot right after you graduate, even if you think you can put a hunk of money down or still afford the payment. You have to take the same roads to work, and you'll still get there whether you're driving a Kia or a BMW. Figure out what you can reasonably afford with payment, insurance, fuel, and maintenance, and still look for something just below that monthly amount."*
>
> — Portia, Florida Atlantic University, Class of 2002

Don't be ashamed if you can't afford what others can. Life is a marathon, and if you work hard and trust the process, you'll get what you want. If that means taking the bus until you can afford a used car with a one-time payment instead of a new car you're paying for monthly, do it."

— Dave, Ramapo College, Class of 2011

IF YOU'RE BUYING NEW, SHOULD YOU BUY OR LEASE?

If you decide on a new car, your next decision is whether to buy or lease that car. If you decide to lease the car, you will never actually own it. Essentially, you are "renting" the car for a set number of months, normally around thirty-six months (or three years), at a set monthly price. You are generally restricted on how many miles you can drive. You will pay more per month if you commit to a 12,000 mile/year contract instead of a 10,000 mile/year agreement. Knowing approximately how many miles you'll drive each year will be important in this case, because if you go over your allocated miles, you'll end up paying a certain price for each mile over your preset amount. However, if you only use 8,000 of the 12,000 miles you had available, you could have probably saved money each month by paying less than you're paying for the higher mileage usage.

If I could go back, I would have put money down, negotiated the price down, and owned the car outright. Since I did not, I am now on my third lease and am throwing money away as I drive less than 10k miles a year. When my lease is up in November, I may just purchase a final car."

— Diane, Temple University, Class of 2004

The great news with a lease is that you don't have to put down as large of a down payment (or any at all) to make the monthly payments more bearable. This may be a wise financial choice for a new graduate who may not have tons of savings and is looking for ways to keep their out-of-pocket expenses low when acquiring a new vehicle. Often, a lease will come with some sort of service agreement that covers repairs likely to come up during the first few years of the car's life. This way, if anything major comes up, you won't be on the hook for it. The repairs are included in the lease pricing that, as you may expect, is negotiable. The only thing that is NOT negotiable in a lease agreement is the price you will pay to buy the car after the lease is complete. That is a preset amount that is locked in the moment you sign the agreement papers. The dealership would prefer that you lease the car instead of buying it. They are banking on you returning to the dealership in a few years to return the car and lease another new vehicle. This results in a new sale for the dealership, which helps them hit their monthly goals. If you were to buy the car, chances are you wouldn't be back in for a new car for almost twice as long.

The downside to a lease is you're always going to have a car payment. You will never own a car outright; you will always be paying a certain amount each month. You're not paying toward the ownership of anything and won't have any sort of trade-in if you decide to switch from a lease to purchasing a new or used car.

> *Leasing was a great option for us because the dealership takes care of everything. My husband was in an accident and could give the car back a year later. We didn't have to try to re-sell a car with an accident on its record, which was great. But with a lease, you always have a car payment!"*
>
> - Sarah, James Madison University, Class of 2004

NAVIGATING THE CAR-BUYING EXPERIENCE

I come from a sales background, but even I get skeeved out at the idea of a "used car salesman," so I get it. But not all car sales professionals are bad. I promise! Chris Bennett, a graduate of NADA (National Automotive Dealer Association) who ran two different dealerships for a total of ten years, provided great insight when I asked for his input on how a customer can better understand the car-buying process. I wanted his advice on how to prepare before you walk onto the lot, things to look out for, and gimmicks to ignore. He also shared insights into how car salesmen and dealerships make money, so you're aware of what you're dealing with, ways to get a good deal, things to look out for, and how to navigate the car-buying experience as a whole. Knowing all of this should shed some light on how a customer can be better educated and prepared when walking into a dealership.

The first thing he said to me was to know that "everything is negotiable. The selling price, the amount you put down, the length of the loan, the trade-in value of your current car, the monthly payments, the cost of the warranty. All of it. Often, customers stop at the sticker price. If they can get that cost down, they feel like they've won. And while it's true that they have saved a bit of money, there's more that can be saved."

In 2018, the landscape of how car dealerships and car salesmen were compensated shifted. Car salesmen used to get paid mostly off of commission, which was based on the difference between the invoice price (what the car dealership paid to get the car from the manufacturer) and the retail price (the price you, as the customer, ultimately pays for the car). Even though they still make a commission, the incentive to sell a higher number of cars is more attractive than it previously was. At the end of the day, though, they just want to move the cars off the lots. Whether it's a sale or a lease, they want it gone. Each salesperson and sales team has a quota, and their goal is to do whatever it takes to get rid of a car and hit that quota. When they meet or exceed that number, the manufacturer of the car (Ford, Toyota, Nissan, etc.) provides bonuses to those individuals or sales teams, as well as the dealerships as a whole. Keep this in mind. Ultimately, their goal of selling the car is more important than how much they sell the car for. This is why there is some truth to hitting up a dealership toward the end of the month, where there may be added pressure to move cars off the lot to hit that quota. Perhaps that sales team had a killer month, and maybe they don't need to sell a car to hit their quota. But even if they've already exceeded their quota, they're getting accelerated bonuses for all cars sold above that goal. So there's incentive all the time. January, February, and September are the slowest months at dealerships, so if you've got flexibility, walking in toward the end of one of those three months will be your best opportunity to find a motivated salesperson and, in turn, get the best deal possible.

Chris warns, "Don't be fooled by the advertisements of 'employee pricing' and 'rebates' available. Often when they mention "rebates" on a commercial, those rebates are for specific populations of people. For example, you may hear there's a $2,000 rebate available. Well, that may only be for members of the military. Or perhaps that $2,000 is made up of a $1,000 loyalty rebate (for those who have already purchased from that dealership before) and a separate $1,000 for senior citizens." If you walk into that dealership, that $2,000 that you were anticipating may not be available to you.

When I asked Chris about his recommendation for a new college grad, he thought a lease would be a great option, especially if you don't have a car to trade in. His logic is that you need to put little money down, far less than you would on a new or used car, and the monthly payment is generally lower. Also, since a lease is always on a new car and often there is a service plan attached to a lease, a new graduate won't need to worry about unexpected repairs that will require out-of-pocket payments. If there's an issue with the car, you just bring it back to the dealership, and the repair is covered.

AVOIDING THE CAR DEALERSHIP ALTOGETHER

Each year, there are more and more online options like CarMax.com and Carvana.com available, where you may not even need to leave your couch to buy a car. Just make sure you're working with a reputable dealer. Not all online sources are created equal. There is also a variety of local buy/trade groups on social media sites and forums where you could potentially find your next car, but beware: the less formal the group, the less protection you'll have against fraud. You could end up buying a lemon. Since I know jack shit about cars, I'm okay paying a slight premium to buy a car from a dealership where I know that I'm protected with warranties, car history reports, etc. There's a price to pay for peace of mind. You need to determine yours and factor that into your decision-making criteria.

At the end of the day, you need to make the choice that makes the most sense for you. You are an adult. You can spend your money on whatever you want, and if you want to buy new, then do it. If you'd rather buy used, then do that. And if you decide to forgo the car altogether and piece together transportation in other ways, that works too!

Key takeaways:

1. DETERMINE IF YOU NEED A CAR OR HAVE OTHER MODES OF TRANSPORTATION AT YOUR DISPOSAL. THINK ABOUT WHERE YOU LIVE, WHERE YOU WORK, AND WHAT'S NEARBY.

2. IF YOU NEED A CAR AND CURRENTLY HAVE ONE, THE BEST MOVE MAY BE TO KEEP WHAT YOU'VE GOT, ESPECIALLY IF THERE'S NO CAR PAYMENT ATTACHED TO IT.

3. IF YOU NEED TO SHOP FOR A CAR, DETERMINE YOUR BUDGET AND DECIDE WHETHER USED OR NEW—AND, IF NEW, WHETHER BUYING OR LEASING—FITS YOUR SITUATION.

4. KNOW THAT BOTH YOU AND THE CAR SALESMAN WANT YOU TO LEAVE WITH A CAR. ULTIMATELY, YOU SHARE THE SAME GOAL.

5. BE ARMED WITH KNOWLEDGE WHEN WALKING INTO A DEALERSHIP: KNOW HOW THE SALES TEAM IS COMPENSATED, BE MINDFUL THAT ADVERTISED REBATES AND PROMOTIONS DON'T ALWAYS APPLY TO YOU, AND, WHEN POSSIBLE, AIM TO VISIT THE DEALERSHIP TOWARD THE END OF THE MONTH OR AT ESPECIALLY SLOW TIMES DURING THE YEAR.

Chapter Six

HOW DO I MANAGE THE MONEY I'M MAKING?

So you've secured a job and a salary of, let's say, $40k, $50k, or $60k. But you may be wondering where all of your money is going and why you're barely scraping by. I've been there! I had never made more money in my life just after graduating, yet I felt like I was at the risk of going negative in my checking account daily. It took me a while to fully understand the difference between my expected weekly salary and what I took home in my weekly paycheck. And once the money got deposited in my account, I couldn't understand how it disappeared so quickly. For most individuals, the two biggest culprits are variable or unexpected expenses and taxes, two things that you cannot avoid, no matter how hard you try.

"Where the hell is all of the money going?" That was a question I asked myself almost immediately after becoming a full-time employee. My starting salary was $42,000. That's right, $42,000! Holy shit! That was a ton of money, more than I would need to start my life in San Diego. Or so I thought. I quickly learned that the $42,000 I thought I'd bring home is just the starting line. That annual salary makes a lot of pit stops before the money hits your bank account. Let's go through that super-disappointing journey together, shall we?

PRE-TAX DEDUCTIONS

Most companies offer an option to take some of your pre-tax money to save for retirement and pay for your own health benefits (that is, if Mom and Dad haven't cut you off yet). We will dive deep into retirement savings options, but before we do that, let's tackle health benefits first.

When a company offers "benefits," that often means you are part of their group plan, which gives you discounted premiums to join. A few companies pay these premiums for you, but most don't. Most of the time, you, the employee, are contributing a little from each paycheck. Let's say, for example's sake, that these cost you $200/month. That's $2,400 a year. Let's also assume you're following the wise advice of many financial advisors and have a 401k set up. Let's also say you put the recommended 10 percent of your annual salary ($42,000) away for savings. That's another $4,200 that's being taken out over the course of a year. If there are no other deductions taken out (Health Savings Account, Transportation Benefits, etc.) you are having $6,600 taken out of your paycheck before it gets taxed. That means that, according to the IRS, your taxable income is actually $35,400 ($42,000 - $6,600). Let's illustrate this a bit:

STARTING SALARY	$42,000	YOUR ANNUAL SALARY
Pre-tax money taken out for retirement	-$4,200	10 percent of your annual salary
Pre-tax money taken out for healthcare premiums	-$2,400	$200/month x 12 months
TAXABLE INCOME	$35,400	What you actually pay taxes on

Tax Brackets and Rates, 2020

Rate	For Single Individuals, Taxable Income Over	For Married Individuals Filing Joint Returns, Taxable Income Over	For Heads of Households, Taxable Income Over
10%	$0	$0	$0
12%	$9,875	$19,750	$14,100
22%	$40,125	$80,250	$53,700
24%	$85,525	$171,050	$85,500
32%	$163,300	$326,600	$163,300
35%	$207,350	$414,700	$207,350
37%	$518,400	$622,050	$518,400

Source: Internal Revenue Service

Based on your taxable income, you fall into the 12 percent tax bracket. Tax brackets are marginal, which means that every time you enter a new tax bracket, the extra money you make is now taxed at the new level. For example, the first $9,874 you make will be taxed at 10 percent. Then all the money between $9,875 and $40,124 is taxed at 12 percent. Keep in mind, your salary may be $42,000 but your TAXABLE income is $35,400, so you would be in the 12 percent bracket. If your taxable income was over $40,125, you'd then be taxed at 22 percent, which is a big difference from the 12 percent that you're currently in. As you can see, the more you make, the more taxes you'll pay. Fair? It probably depends on your political views. Fact? Yes, this is just how it is.

Based on this tax bracket, your income tax for a full year would be $4,050.52. That means that over the course of the year, you owe the government that much money. (Keep in mind, there are state taxes. And sometimes local taxes. And a bunch of other deductions that hit your check before that check hits your bank account. For example's sake, we'll ignore them for now, but in real life? Yeah, not something you can ignore).

So, that $35,400 now drops to $31,349. That number feels a lot different than the $42,000 you were expecting to take home.

Okay, more pictures coming up. Chances are, you've already been contributing some of this amount with each paycheck. Let's assume that you get paid bi-weekly and are withholding

$155.79/paycheck; come tax day, you won't get a refund, and you won't owe anything either (because $155.79 x 26 paychecks = $4,050.52. But if you claim "0" when filling out your initial tax forms with that company, and more than $155.79 is being withheld, then you essentially have overpaid the government and will get the difference back. If you withhold less from each paycheck (by claiming a higher number on your W-4), then you may have underpaid; if so, you'll owe money.

*Numbers are rounded to the nearest dollar for sake of example.

WHAT YOU EXPECT	$42,000/ 52 weeks	$807/week	Sweet!
WHAT YOU ACTUALLY GET	$31,349/ 52 weeks	$602/week**	Not as sweet.

**Use this amount to create a budget

Now, keep in mind, you are putting away $4,200 a year for your retirement, which will compound over time. One of the best pieces of advice I received early in my career was to start saving for retirement right away. Start with a small amount of your paycheck, and don't touch it. I didn't feel like I had any extra money to put away at the time, but I'm glad that I did it. I'm glad that I developed a savings habit and learned to live on 90% of my paycheck from day one. Initially, I told myself that I would save more when I made more. Unlikely. Savings is a habit, and even if it's not 10 percent now, start somewhere and make sure you're saving a little bit of money each week.

There have been full books written on how money compounds over time, but the quick way of explaining it is that, over time, your initial $4,200 will grow and earn interest. Then, what you put in the following year, plus the initial deposit and the interest earned from that initial deposit, will "compound" (grow) and make even more interest. Year over year, if you structure it correctly, you can end up as a multi-millionaire when you retire. The cool thing about this is that as your income grows due to raises and promotions and possibly switching companies, if you've kept your deduction at 10 percent, you'll be saving more and more money. By the time you're making $100,000, you're putting $10,000 away each year!

It may be silly to start thinking about retirement when you've barely scratched the surface of your adult life, but small, smart decisions now will benefit you greatly in the future. We'll dive deeper into the idea of long-term savings in the next chapter, but for now, it's important that you're aware of what you're making currently and best practices when it comes to managing it.

One tip I got early in my career was to open up an 'out of sight, out of mind' savings account that was not easily accessible and make regular, weekly contributions. This was such great advice that I still use it to this day. One thing I would change if I could go back would be to max out my 401k contributions on an annual basis from day one. I didn't do this the first few years I was working (I only put in I think 3-5 percent). In hindsight, I wish I had maxed out; it would not have been that much more out of each paycheck, and I think it would have made a somewhat sizable difference at this point."

– Kara, Pennsylvania State University, Class of 2010

BUDGETING

Although the idea of creating and following a budget may seem tedious and unnecessary, there is real value that comes from working through this exercise. If you have a better understanding of where your money is currently going, you're able to make adjustments in order to support both your needs and your wants. Having this control of your money and spending habits will allow you to work toward your financial goals, including establishing savings, paying off debt, and still leaving room for you to enjoy all that life has to offer. If done properly, following a monthly budget will allow you to allocate your money toward unsexy things like rent, insurance, and utilities as well as fun things like eating out, entertainment, and travel.

Often we can find "extra" money in our monthly budget by tracking some of the mindless spending that we aren't even aware of. A cup of coffee here and there or that extra round at the bar can add up to larger amounts when tracked over the month or year. That's not to say that you need to cut these expenses totally out of your life; I like coffee and adult beverages as much as the next person and spend money on both of them regularly. However, it is important to have a handle on how often you are spending money on these items and decide if some of the money you're spending would be better spent in other areas of your life.

> *I made a great salary, but I spent money way too frivolously as a young professional. I wish I had followed a budget (even a generous one) and paid off my student loans more quickly. Best practice: make a plan to pay off loans within a certain time period (i.e. two to three years), figure out how much you have to pay per month to make that happen, and then stick to it!"*
>
> - Sarah, Boston University, Class of 2005

5 STEPS TOWARD CREATING A BUDGET

1. **Identify all monthly income.** This amount should include all money that you receive on a monthly basis. Most companies will pay you bi-weekly, so if you don't have a commission as part of your income, this number will be easy to calculate. Work off of your net income or "take-home" income. Once all of your taxes have been taken out and any deductions from your paycheck have

been removed, what's left? We already talked about how your salary isn't really what you see in each paycheck, so working off of that higher number will throw off this whole exercise. Remember: use your post-deduction weekly income when budgeting. Apart from your full-time job, do you have any other income? A side hustle? Do you bartend or babysit? Do you sell things online? Consign clothes through Poshmark or ThredUp? It's up to you to decide whether or not these factor into your budget. It also depends on how consistent this number is or how large it is. For years, I sold stuff on eBay, mostly clothes and vintage PEZ dispensers (yes, I had an aggressive collection; we're talking in the 1000's). I made a couple hundred dollars here and there from those sales. Maybe some years, it added up to $1000, but to me, it wasn't enough to include in my budget. If that money came in, it just padded my checking account a bit and ended up becoming "fun" money. If you have a legit second stream of income, throw it in there. If not, stick with just the guaranteed income from your full-time job.

2. **Make a list of all of your regular monthly expenses.** This amount should include all fixed expenses (rent, car payment, student loan payment, insurance payments, savings disbursements, etc.) as well as ones that are generally around the same amount (utilities, cell phone, gas, etc.).

3. **Make a list of all of your variable expenses.** This amount includes all expenses that may vary from month to month. While they may generally stay around the same amount, you may see spikes in certain areas in a given month depending on what's happening in your life. Consider expenses such as credit card payments, food, entertainment, travel, car repair, charity donations, gifts, medical expenses, clothing, and about 4,589 other things you're not even thinking about right now. Don't be ultra-conservative with these numbers. In fact, before calculating this number, I'd recommend letting a month

go by and spend how you normally would. During that time, you'll see your spending habits and also notice some of the little things that may have otherwise slipped your mind. Or, if you're ready to create a budget today, pull up your most recent bank and credit card statements and do some investigating. A good rule of thumb is to take your total expenses and increase it by 10 percent to 15 percent. So if you expect your variable monthly expenses to be $2,000, round it up to $2,200 or slightly more for the "buffer." This will account for some of the variable expenses that may get a little out of control for that particular month.

4. **Separate needs and wants.** This will be a very personal exercise. It's clear that not everyone *needs* cable or a going-out budget as much as money set aside for rent or insurances, but for you, it may be important to allocate money for both. You may deem one thing as a need and be willing to sacrifice in another area. When you think about your spending, ask yourself whether you "want it" or "need it."

5. **Do the math.** Subtract how much you spend each month (the lists created from steps 2 and 3) from how much you earn each month (the amount you reached in step 1). While you're doing this calculation, say a quick prayer that the result is not a negative number. If it is, you've got to go back and look at your expenses, both fixed and variable, and see where you can cut some corners and reel in spending. And if you find out that you can't adjust the spending, you may have to start looking for a second job or income stream in order to maintain your standard of living.

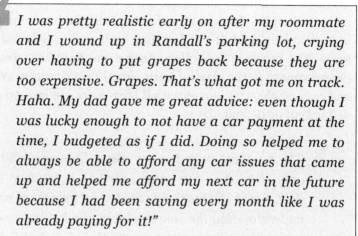

I was pretty realistic early on after my roommate and I wound up in Randall's parking lot, crying over having to put grapes back because they are too expensive. Grapes. That's what got me on track. Haha. My dad gave me great advice: even though I was lucky enough to not have a car payment at the time, I budgeted as if I did. Doing so helped me to always be able to afford any car issues that came up and helped me afford my next car in the future because I had been saving every month like I was already paying for it!"

- Maria, University of Missouri, Class of 2010

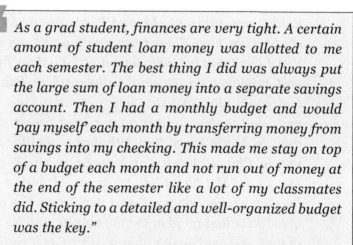

As a grad student, finances are very tight. A certain amount of student loan money was allotted to me each semester. The best thing I did was always put the large sum of loan money into a separate savings account. Then I had a monthly budget and would 'pay myself' each month by transferring money from savings into my checking. This made me stay on top of a budget each month and not run out of money at the end of the semester like a lot of my classmates did. Sticking to a detailed and well-organized budget was the key."

- Kyle, Tulane University, Class of 2015

STUDENT LOANS

According to a 2019 *Forbes* article, student loan debt is at an all-time high. It's affecting not only recent college grads but also graduates of all ages and demographics. Right now, there are 45 million borrowers in the United States who collectively owe north of $1.5 trillion. Mortgage debt still makes up the largest collective personal debt for most of the U.S., but in second place is student loan debt. It's higher than both credit cards and auto loans. The Institute for College Access and Success states that the borrowers in the class of 2017 owe almost $30,000 apiece, and as a whole, 11.4 percent of all borrowers are in a 90+ day delinquent or default status.

> *The toughest part for me about finances (and the only debt that I've ever carried) is student loan debt. I took out buttloads of student loans, not really understanding the consequences of what that would mean later down the line. To this day, I still have about $124,000 in student loan debt, which makes me want to throw up. I didn't get my first credit card until I was 28 years old, and I only use it to build credit right now. I don't put anything on my card that I can't pay off that same day. I think as far as best practices go, getting well-versed in finances and continuing to learn where your money goes and what to do with it is a topic most people won't discuss. I once heard that 'Nike has a plan for your money, Chipotle has a plan for your money, Reebok, Macy's, H&M, Chick-fil-A, Apple, etc. all have a plan for your money; do you?' And that hit me like a ton of bricks. I had no plan for my money, and because of that, it would go out almost as fast as it came in. I think we live in a consumer world, and the biggest thing that I've been able to invest in over these last four years is myself, but we need a plan for our time and our money. If we don't tell it where to go, it will tell us where to go."*
>
> - Brilynn, NYIT, Class of 2009

Student loan debt is my number one issue. At the time that I took out student loans, I was eighteen years old with no real financial experience or understanding of interest rates, etc. I made the horrible mistake of paying double to go to out-of-state school and went through Wells Fargo to take out private student loans with an outrageous interest rate. No one ever explained to me what I was doing. So, sitting here today I have $86K in student loan debt with a MINIMUM payment of $1,000/month for the next fifteen years. It's a disaster. Biggest financial mistake I've made. As far as lessons learned, I think Dave Ramsey's books and teachings have really helped me understand money and budgeting better. Aside from student loans and our mortgage, my husband and I are debt-free."

- Taylor, University of Kansas, Class of 2015

SHOULD YOU REFINANCE YOUR STUDENT LOANS?

Depending on the loan that you took out, you may already be making monthly payments, or you may still be in a grace period, which means you aren't making monthly payments quite yet. Many loans allow you to defer payments until six months after you graduate, but make no mistake: the loans will be waiting for you, as will the interest that has been generated from the loan.

If you do have private or federal student loan debt, it's likely private lenders have contacted you with deals to refinance your loan. Refinancing involves replacing one or more of your student loans with better loan terms from one of these private lenders. The goal is to lower your interest rate, which will reduce the overall cost of the loan as well as the monthly payments. These private lenders include banks, online lenders, and credit unions. Each lender offers its own rates, so it's important to shop around and see what the best deal is for you.

Often there are savings involved in refinancing, so if you've got a decent credit score, this should be an option you strongly consider. Before deciding whether to refinance or not, keep these things in mind:

1. **What's the new interest rate you'd be getting, and what's the new term duration?** Not every lender is the same, so ensure that you'll be saving money by going with this option. You should notice a difference in your monthly payment as well as savings for the loan as a whole. Make sure that you're actually saving money by refinancing. If you refinance at a lower rate but over a longer period of time, you may notice a decrease in your monthly payment but may pay more overall due to accruing interest.

2. **Do you have steady income and employment?** If so, and your credit is in a decent spot, you should find yourself eligible for a reduced repayment rate. If you haven't secured a job yet and/or have a poor credit score, you may find it more difficult to get a reduced rate, as the lender will want to see proof of income. As far as your credit goes, a score of 700 or more is considered good, and 620 - 700 is considered average. If you're not there yet, waiting until your score increases and you've got a more consistent source of income can help you get a better rate at a later time.

3. **How much remaining debt do you have?** As a recent grad, you may have tens of thousands of dollars of debt in front of you. In this case, a refinance option may make sense. But if you only have a small amount of debt to pay off, refinancing may not be worth it. You may save a bit of money, but your credit score may be negatively affected by this refinance. This is especially important to consider if you're also in the market for another loan or mortgage, as too many inquiries into

your creditworthiness (at your request) can lower your credit score.

PROS	CONS
Potential for savings over the life of the loan	Applying for refinance can have a negative effect on your credit score
Decrease in monthly payments	Longer term loans have the potential to increase the lifetime cost of the loan
Single payment each month and flexible payment terms	By refinancing federal loans, you waive your rights to cancellation or loan forgiveness programs you may be eligible for
Option of dropping previous co-signer from loan	

LOAN FORGIVENESS PROGRAM OPTIONS

If you do not have any private loans, you may be able to consolidate all federal loans into one monthly payment. If, even after consolidation, you're unable meet the minimum payments, you may also be able to explore some of the programs available to forgive a portion—or all—of your loan amount. Specifically, you may be eligible for one of the following forgiveness programs.

1. **Public Service Loan Forgiveness:** This is restricted to employees of federal, state, or local government organizations and certain non-profits.

2. **Teacher Loan Forgiveness:** Reserved for teachers who have taught full time in a low-income school or education service agency for a minimum of five consecutive years.

3. **Perkins Loan Cancellations:** Also for teachers, specifically for those who work in low-income schools or teach children with disabilities. Other teachers who may qualify are those who teach math, science, foreign languages, or other fields considered as having a shortage of qualified teachers.

LONG-TERM SAVINGS

Remember when I told you that the $1 you were about to spend, if saved instead, could be $5 in the future? How is that possible? Well, it's based on the Compound Effect, a theory that small, seemingly insignificant decisions build on each other, creating a larger result at some point in the future. The book by the same name, written by Darren Hardy, is a recommended read for everyone, regardless of the industry you're in and the goals you have. It's a great way to look at your current habits and find the keys to success in your daily routine.

Before I heard about the book, I heard about the concept of the compound effect when it came to money. When I was sixteen, I was lucky enough to attend a program called Eagle University (www.eagleuniversity.org), which gives high school- and college-aged students a seven-year career head start on life. Over the course of a few days, you learn how to set your life direction, ask for what you want, gain confidence, and learn how to set and go after goals. Additionally, you learn some good life lessons about how to perform in school, how to interact with others better by understanding personality differences, and financial habits that should start as soon as you're old enough to earn your first paycheck. It was there where I learned about how money compounds and that savings is truly a habit. No matter how much you can save, whether it's $1/month or $1000/month, you've got to start now. Time is on your side. If you wait to save until you have more money, you're going to miss out on some serious cash in the future.

WHO WANTS TO BE A MILLIONAIRE?

Age	INVESTOR A		INVESTOR B	
	Contri-bution	Year-End Value	Contri-bution	Year-End Value
8	-0-	-0-	-0-	-0-
9	-0-	-0-	-0-	-0-
10	-0-	-0-	-0-	-0-
11	-0-	-0-	-0-	-0-
12	-0-	-0-	-0-	-0-
13	-0-	-0-	-0-	-0-
14	-0-	-0-	-0-	-0-
15	-0-	-0-	-0-	-0-
16	-0-	-0-	-0-	-0-
17	-0-	-0-	-0-	-0-
18	-0-	-0-	-0-	-0-
19	-0-	-0-	2,000	2,200
20	-0-	-0-	2,000	4,620
21	-0-	-0-	2,000	7,282
22	-0-	-0-	2,000	10,210
23	-0-	-0-	2,000	13,431
24	-0-	-0-	2,000	16,974
25	-0-	-0-	2,000	20,872
26	2,000	2,200	-0-	22,959
27	2,000	4,620	-0-	25,255
28	2,000	7,282	-0-	27,780
29	2,000	10,210	-0-	30,558
30	2,000	13,431	-0-	33,614
31	2,000	16,974	-0-	36,976
32	2,000	20,872	-0-	40,673
33	2,000	25,159	-0-	44,741
34	2,000	29,875	-0-	49,215
35	2,000	35,062	-0-	54,136
36	2,000	40,769	-0-	59,550
37	2,000	47,045	-0-	65,505
38	2,000	53,950	-0-	72,055
39	2,000	61,545	-0-	79,261
40	2,000	69,899	-0-	87,187
41	2,000	79,089	-0-	95,905
42	2,000	89,198	-0-	105,496
43	2,000	100,318	-0-	116,045
44	2,000	112,550	-0-	127,650
45	2,000	126,005	-0-	140,415
46	2,000	140,805	-0-	154,456
47	2,000	157,086	-0-	169,902
48	2,000	174,995	-0-	186,892
49	2,000	194,694	-0-	205,581
50	2,000	216,364	-0-	226,140
51	2,000	240,200	-0-	248,754
52	2,000	266,420	-0-	273,629
53	2,000	295,262	-0-	300,992
54	2,000	326,988	-0-	331,091
55	2,000	361,887	-0-	364,200
56	2,000	400,276	-0-	400,620
57	2,000	442,503	-0-	440,682
58	2,000	488,953	-0-	484,750
59	2,000	540,049	-0-	533,225
60	2,000	596,254	-0-	586,548
61	2,000	658,079	-0-	645,203
62	2,000	726,087	-0-	709,723
63	2,000	800,896	-0-	780,695
64	2,000	883,185	-0-	858,765
65	2,000	973,704	-0-	944,641
Less Total Invested:		(80,000)		(14,000)
Equals Net Earnings:		893,704		930,641
Money Grew:		11-fold		66-fold

Want to be a millionaire when you retire but don't want to start saving until you have more money? I understand - perhaps you are living close to paycheck to paycheck or you'd rather spend your disposable income on items and experiences that will bring you instant gratification. However, I'd urge you not to wait to start creating a habit around savings. Time is on your side if you start working towards an annual investment goal as soon as possible.

Take a look at this study from a company called Market Logic, taken from a famous Richard Russell article called "Rich Dad, Poor Dad." The study assumes that investor "A" decides to start investing at age 26. Each year he contributes $2,000, which equates to roughly $167/month. This investor then makes contributions of $2,000 every year until reaching the age of 65. In total, investor A contributes a total of 40 times - $80,000 in total contributions. When he reaches age 65, the account has $973,704 in it. After deducting the $80,000 in contributions made over the years, that results in net earnings of 893,704. Not bad, right?

Want to know something even cooler than that? What if you started investing at age 19 instead of age 26? Take a look at investor "B." Assuming the same return, you would have had to contribute $2,000 a year for only seven years to come close to the million dollar mark. In total, you would have invested $14,000 and grew that into $944,641. When you deduct your $14,000 that was invested, you've earned a total of $930,641.

So not only are you contributing about $66,000 less over the course of your lifetime, you're walking away with more once you reach retirement age.

In more simplified terms: if you start saving sooner, you can save less and end up with more.

Compounding makes the sum of your account grow at a faster rate than simple interest, because not only are you earning returns on your actual investment, you're also earning money on the money you've already made on your investment. As a result, your wealth starts to snowball over time. This means that you don't have to save as much for as long in order to reach the same end goal.

The bottom line? The faster you start saving, the faster you can start taking advantage of compound interest...so what are you waiting for? Share your goals with a financial advisor to find out the best vehicles for retirement savings. As mentioned in the "benefits" part of finding a job, many employers offer a 401k program, and many offer to match some of your contributions as well. They may match up to a certain percentage or dollar amount of whatever you contribute. This is free money; take advantage of it!

My most recent employer offered a pretty weak match program, but I still took advantage of it. They matched the first $500 of what I put in and also matched 50 percent of the second $500 I contributed. Essentially, that meant that if I put $1000 in my 401k each year through pre-tax deductions, the company would add $750 to my plan. Where else can you turn $1000 into $1750 overnight? Well, I can think of a few places (Vegas, Atlantic City, possibly a drug ring), but where can you *legally* get that type of return? Do what you can to maximize any company matching program that's offered. There are some great ones out there right now. If your company doesn't offer a great matching plan, you can still contribute to their plan and then seek outside programs (a second 401k, Roth IRA, or traditional IRA) through a financial advisor. Just please don't keep it in a checking account! You want it out of sight, out of mind, growing and compounding over time.

Key Takeaways:

1. CREATE AND FOLLOW A BUDGET. DOING SO WILL ENSURE YOU'RE PREPARED TO MEET ALL OF YOUR NEEDS AND STILL BE ABLE TO ENJOY YOUR "WANTS."

2. IF YOU HAVE STUDENT LOAN DEBT, LOOK INTO REFINANCING OPTIONS TO POSSIBLY LOWER YOUR INTEREST, MONTHLY PAYMENTS, AND THE OVERALL PRICE OF THE LOAN.

3. THE TIME TO START SAVING IS NOW. SET AUTOMATIC SAVINGS UP SO YOUR MONEY CAN START EARNING INTEREST, COMPOUNDING OVER TIME.

Chapter Seven

HOW DO I CUT BACK ON MY VARIABLE EXPENSES?

By creating your monthly budget, you should have a better understanding of your fixed and variable costs each month. Rent, insurance payments, and student loan payments are all fixed amounts and, no matter how hard you pray, those aren't going down—at least not anytime soon. If you're finding yourself tight on cash at the end of each month and you're not up for moving to a cheaper place to live, the only way to lower your monthly expenses is to dig into the variable spending that happens each month. Make small tweaks to how much you spend in each of the following categories and you might feel a little less strapped moving forward.

FEED YOURSELF WELL WITHOUT DRAINING YOUR BANK ACCOUNT

As recent graduates, you might be cooking for yourself for the first time. You've got to navigate a kitchen and make smart choices on the go, both of which cost money. Remember the good ol' days when you could swipe a card at a dining facility on campus or a local spot nearby and you got food, a latte, or even a few glasses of wine for "free"? Well, the days of "dining dollars" are over. You can swipe a card, but that card is attached to your bank account. You are dealing with actual dollars now.

One of the largest monthly variable costs a new graduate can have is the amount of money they spend on food and beverages. The great news is that this is also one of the easiest areas to control. If you're searching for ways to decrease your monthly spending, looking at what you eat and drink regularly can reveal a lot. Many think it's cheaper to buy crappy food than healthy food that fuels you. And while this is true sometimes, eating well doesn't always mean you need to spend more. Even if you don't like to cook (me!) and aren't good at it (also me!), there are still ways to fuel your body with the right things and not break the bank in order to do so.

MEAL PLANNING

Have you ever had grand plans for what you'll cook, and then went to the store to stock up on everything you'd need— only to throw half of it out later in the week? Been there! On the days that I worked later than expected, the last thing I wanted to do was start prepping a meal from scratch. Going out or ordering take-out was so much more convenient. Those decisions negatively impacted me in two ways: not only did I spend money on the meal when I went out or ordered in, but I also didn't use the food I'd already purchased. A double loss for the wallet and the waistline.

Planning out your meals each week is helpful for many reasons. Doing this allows you to take a step back and look at the week as a whole. Do you have two lunch meetings and one dinner with a friend? Great, then you don't need to worry about planning those meals. But assuming you're eating three meals each day, you've still got eighteen other meals to think about. If you know you'll have a late meeting on Tuesday, plan for take-out that night. Don't pretend that you'll come home after your long day and long commute and start cooking. Work that into your plan. Save the cooking for a night when you know you'll be home with more time to prepare a meal. If you live with a roommate, try to coordinate with him/her as well. Perhaps you can take turns cooking or double up the effort on a meal so the prep time isn't so bad.

Think about meals that can last more than one day or bulk prep so you can take care of a few meals in one shot. Grilled chicken is always something I have on hand. If you have it for dinner on Monday, throw some of the leftovers on your salad for Tuesday or add some different sauce and a new veggie and it becomes a quick dinner to whip up when you're working late. Making one big batch of rice or quinoa on Sunday or Monday also helps save time later in the week. Cooking one serving of rice or five servings or rice takes the same amount of time. Spending thirty minutes doing it once at the start of the week and then one minute of re-heating when you are ready to eat is a better use of your precious time, especially on a weeknight. Time is the only resource you can't ever get back, but there are little tricks you can do to save yourself some time, thus feeling like you have more of it.

Once your meals are prepped for the week, you can transfer the necessary ingredients to a grocery list. Then, when you go shopping, only buy the things on your list. This seems basic, but I'm telling you, the few dollars here and there that you waste by over-purchasing adds up. Once you're home from the store, divide up the bulk items you bought into easy-to-grab portions to save you time later. Break up the bag of baby carrots into individual servings and pop into reusable storage containers or—the less-environmentally-friendly option—small plastic baggies. If they're all ready to go, you're more likely to reach for one on those healthy options for a quick snack now or on your way out the door. Additionally, you can find tons of food available in pre-portioned servings, but they're more costly. Items such as fruits, veggies, eggs, yogurts, hummus, and cheese are among some of the many options you can find in ready-to-go packaging. You've got to decide if the added cost to your grocery bill is worth the convenience.

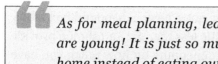

> *As for meal planning, learn how to cook when you are young! It is just so much better for you to eat at home instead of eating out all the time or doing take-out. Not only will you save money, but when you cook at home it is generally a lot healthier as well."*
>
> - Eric, University of California, San Diego, Class of 2006.

Despite what you may think, all of your groceries don't need to be organic and purchased from Whole Foods in order to maintain a healthy diet. I probably have close to 100 donuts a year (not an exaggeration—not sure if I'm proud or ashamed. I take it back; I'm super proud of that shit!). Even after this admission, I still consider myself healthy. As I write this, my primary source of income is as a Health and Fitness Coach so yeah, it may seem a little off to hear about my donut obsession. However, I know how to make mostly good decisions when it comes to my health, and when I go off the rails a bit, I know what I need to do to reel it back in.

PURCHASE FOODS THAT ARE AFFORDABLE AND FUEL YOUR BODY

Here are ten items that you can work into your meal plan that cost $2 or less per serving. Many of these can be made in batches to save time later in the week.

1. **Brown rice:** It's great for side dishes, protein bowls, stir-fries, and adding to soups or stews. A 1-pound bag is usually around $2 and contains ten servings. That's $0.20/serving. Can't get much cheaper than that. Each serving of rice contains 170 calories, 4 grams of protein, and 2 grams of fiber.

2. **Whole-wheat pasta:** There are many different kinds of pasta available that provide more nutrition than the standard white-flour-based version. Whole-wheat pasta

is one version that, to me, tastes the most similar and doesn't cost much more. Top with some grilled chicken or another protein, jarred sauce or garlic and oil, and veggies if you'd like, and you've got a meal. A 1-pound box of dry pasta usually costs a little less than $2 and should provide five to seven servings, depending on how much you have per meal. That translates to about $0.25 cents per serving, and the shelf life on pasta is long, so you don't need to worry about it expiring before you finish the box. Each serving of whole-wheat pasta contains about 200 calories, 7 grams of protein (more if you buy a protein-enriched version), and 6 grams of fiber.

3. **Whole-wheat bread:** Packing your lunch and bringing it to work is a much more affordable option than grabbing lunch out each day. Bread can be used for sandwiches and also as part of a healthy breakfast in the mornings. Store-brand wheat bread will run you around $2.00 to $2.50 and provide you with twenty-two slices, enough to make eleven sandwiches. Assuming the price of a loaf of bread is $2.50, which breaks down to $0.11/slice. So for $0.22, you've got yourself bookends to a sandwich and also approximately 120 calories, 6 grams of protein, and 3 grams of fiber.

4. **Non-fat/low-fat Greek yogurt:** Greek yogurt is a great protein-packed option for a quick breakfast or snack throughout the day. You can add it to smoothies, top it with fruit and honey, or use it as the base for a homemade parfait. Although you can buy Greek yogurt in a larger container to save a bit more money, usually you can find one of the popular brands (Chobani, Fage, etc.) on sale for around $1/each. Each 6-oz. serving will contain roughly 150 calories and 14 grams of protein.

5. **Old-fashioned oats:** I used to grab an oatmeal at a little deli down the street from my office in Manhattan. By the time I added some brown sugar and berries on top, it ended up costing me just shy of $5, which is about

what a 42-ounce container of dry oats usually costs. Meanwhile, I was paying that for a 6-ounce cup! Was it more convenient? Sure. But if I was really keeping costs in mind, I could have made this snack at home, and it would have cost me about $0.20/serving. Even when I add brown sugar and berries, making it at home is a more economical option. A serving of most brands of oats will contain about 150 calories, 5 grams of protein, and 4 grams of fiber.

6. **Frozen vegetables:** When possible, I always prefer buying fresh veggies. But they cost more and rot faster. If I know that I'm definitely going to use them within a few days of purchasing them, I will buy fresh. Additionally, I always keep a few bags of frozen veggies in my freezer. They are great for stir-fries, side dishes, or adding to soups and stews. One cup of veggies will cost you around $0.25. You can even stick with organic frozen veggies and pay just a tad bit more. A bag of mixed veggies should last you about 6 servings and will contain about 100 calories, 4 grams of protein, 6 grams of fiber, and over 100 percent of the Recommended Daily Value of Vitamin A.

7. **Fresh bagged/boxed spinach:** These are great for making quick salads, adding to egg dishes, or serving as a side dish. If you're using it as the base of a salad, you'll probably use three or four cups, which will end up costing you about $1 depending on how much you purchased the spinach for. A 9-ounce package of washed spinach should sell for a little shy of $3, and if you get close to the end of the shelf life, you could always freeze what's left and use it in smoothies at a later date. Four cups contain 20 calories, 2 grams of fiber, 160 percent of the Recommended Daily Value of Vitamin A, and almost half of the Daily Value for Vitamin C and Folic Acid.

8. **Canned tuna:** Remember those slices of bread from earlier? Throw some canned tuna between them and

you've got yourself an easy lunch. Also try swapping the mayo for plain Greek yogurt or avocado to keep it even healthier. Or throw it on top of that spinach salad you just theoretically made in the previous example. A can of chunk white albacore in water will cost you about $1.40, while solid white albacore will be closer to $2.00. Having said that, I always keep my eyes out for sales. Often they go on sale and are closer to $1/each. The shelf life on these is long, so stock up when they're on sale and you've got a cheap, convenient option just waiting for you in your pantry. A serving of tuna is going to provide you with a ton of protein—13 grams—and only 60 calories. Plus, you'll get some good Omega 3 fatty acids, which have numerous health benefits, including lowering blood pressure and reducing the likelihood of heart attack and stroke.

9. **Eggs/egg substitute:** Having eggs on hand is great for a ton of reasons. First, it's a cheap, healthy breakfast. You can scramble the eggs, make an omelet or frittata, or hard-boil a few ahead of time to keep on hand for a protein-packed, on-the-go snack. I also like using egg substitute in a stir-fry or fried rice when I'm craving an Asian-style meal. A dozen eggs will cost you around $3 or $4, and an egg substitute will be in a similar range for a 16-oz. container. If you use two eggs (or the equivalent of the substitute) as a serving, you'll end up spending around $0.70 per serving. Plus, you're only consuming 30 calories while getting 6 grams of protein.

10. **Canned beans/dry lentils:** There are so many varieties out there, with black beans, refried beans, kidney beans, and pinto beans being some of more popular and versatile ones. Each can of beans will probably cost right around $1 and should yield two servings. Beans can be used in soups, as a side dish, or as a protein option, because each serving contains anywhere between 6 and 8 grams of protein (depending on which type of bean you select). Lentils are a pretty user-friendly bean because you can cook them quickly without pre-soaking. You can

buy a 1-pound bag for around $1.50, which yields about 13 servings. They expand as they cook, so that little bag will produce more than you may think! That comes out to around $0.12/serving, and you'll consume 150 calories, 10 grams of protein, and 11 grams of fiber.

SET UP YOUR KITCHEN WITH THINGS YOU WILL USE OFTEN

If you walk into a Bed Bath & Beyond, you will see aisles and aisles of gadgets that each serve one particular purpose. You can get a tool that takes the top off of strawberries, an avocado masher, and an apple corer. All of these do their one job very well. However, I think it's safe to assume that your money will be best spent on some essentials that will ensure your kitchen is set up for business. I would also go out on a limb to say that the kitchen in your first home or apartment is on the smaller side. Space may be a hot commodity, so take that into account when you're deciding on whether or not you need those tongs specifically designed to remove toast from the toaster or the mango splitter which, you guessed it, is used to split mangos. Although, if you like mangos, you know what a pain in the ass it is to cut one. Okay, maybe you should get a mango splitter. I'll let you decide.

Below are 20 things that you should have in your kitchen. Obviously, you can get various versions of all of these items; for example, I include a Dutch oven on this list, which you can get on Amazon for $30 or at Williams-Sonoma for $350. Your call. If you stick to entry-level versions of the list below, you should be able to completely set up your kitchen for between $250 and $300. And if you go to Bed Bath & Beyond, please, for the love of God, don't forget those coupons! You probably have 234 of them stacked up somewhere. If not, send me a message, and I'll get one to you. I have about a thousand in my glove compartment right now.

Okay, moving on to your essentials list.

1. **Chef's knife:** Don't worry about the full set of knives that come in a butcher's block. They are expensive and take up a ton of precious counter space, and chances are you won't use them all that often anyway. Save that for your wedding registry, and some relative will buy a set for you and your spouse. A good chef's knife shouldn't cost you more than $50. In addition to the regular knives you probably already have, you should be in pretty good shape.

2. **Cast iron skillet:** This is super versatile: it can be used on the grill, in the oven, and on the stovetop. They can range in price, but you can grab a 10" one on Amazon for around $15/$20 depending on the brand.

3. **Dutch oven:** Another versatile piece that can be used to cook meats and veggies and also taken right to the table for serving. One less dish to clean! Like I mentioned before, Amazon's got a decent starter one for $30.

4. **Sheet pan:** These are needed for baking cookies or fish and are also helpful for roasting veggies. There are many "one-pan" recipes that allow you to cook a whole meal using only that one baking sheet, also making for easy clean up. Plus, it's slim, so storage shouldn't be a big problem. No need to spend more than $10 here.

5. **Tongs:** These serve as an extra set of hands and are great for tossing pastas and salads as well as flipping meat or other hot ingredients. Also around $10 for a sturdy pair.

6. **Silicone utensil set:** Grab one with a variety of spatulas, along with slotted and flat spoons. You can grab a 5- to 7-piece set for under $20.

7. **Large saucepan:** Many people want a full set of saucepans and pots but, while that's nice and convenient, it takes up precious space and costs a ton of money. If you want to keep money and space in mind, grab a large saucepan that holds 3 quarts and comes with a lid. This way, you can still make soups and stews in it and not worry about not having enough storage space. You can snag one for $15-$18.

8. **Cutting board:** Do you need to cut anything? Ever? Then you need a cutting board immediately. I would opt for a different material than wood, and one that can go in the dishwasher would be great too! A large one should be $10 or less.

9. **Kitchen towels:** They come in handy when drying your hands or hand-washed dishes, and you can lay them under a hot pot/pan or use to wipe down countertops. They also add a little color to your kitchen and can easily be thrown in the wash to keep clean. Grab a set of four so you've always got some clean ones on hand. I prefer cotton towels as I think they dry dishes the best; sometimes other materials don't quite absorb the way that the cotton ones do. No need to spend more than $10 on a set of four.

10. **Potholders:** Spending a little more money on these will be worth it—and could keep you out of the ER. There are some available that are glove-shaped that allow for a better grip on pots and pans, unlike some of the oven mitts or traditional potholders. The "Ove Glove" is $20 and totally worth it.

11. **Nonstick skillet:** Although you already have a cast iron pan at your disposal, I'd opt for adding a nonstick pan or two to your arsenal. Cooking and cleaning with these pans is a breeze, and you can grab a set of two pans for $20.

12. **Colander:** One 5-quart colander should be all you need. Draining pastas and rinsing fresh fruits and veggies is super simple when using a colander. I'd expect to spend $7-$10 on one.

13. **Pyrex measuring cup:** You will need a measuring cup that is dedicated to liquids only. Pyrex is a classic brand that is durable and cheap. Five dollars gets you a 1-cup version.

14. **Measuring cups and spoons (for dry ingredients):** You can get a set of four cups and four spoons for less than $10. There are some more elaborate sets, but one that features a cup, one-half cup, one-third cup, and one-quarter cup should be all you need. Same with measuring spoons: one tablespoon, one teaspoon, and then halves of both of those should suffice.

15. **A heat-safe spatula:** Even though you probably got a spatula in the silicone set I suggested earlier, you'll need one that can withstand more heat to use on your stovetop or grill. KitchenAid has a great one, and it's only $9.

16. **Can opener:** While the electric versions are fancy and fun, they cost more and take up more space. Opt for an old-fashioned manual one; they work just as well. This has one purpose and one purpose only, but it's a necessity for sure! $15 should get you a pretty nice one.

17. **Mixing bowls:** Although they often come in a stackable set with various sizes, you really only need a large one to use for mixing ingredients or serving up a big bowl of popcorn. I like the stainless steel ones over the glass ones, but either way, snag one for your kitchen. $10 well spent!

18. **Vegetable peeler:** While you could use a knife to peel a carrot, a peeler will be far easier, and probably safer too! I like the ones with the rubber handle for a better grip. Oxo has a great one for $9.99.

19. **Meat thermometer:** Cooking meat is a little tricky as a beginner. It's critical to make sure that it's cooked to the correct temperature. Many prefer a digital version to an old-school one. There are some good digital options on Amazon for $8-$10.

20. **Bottle opener:** At the end of cooking, you'll need to make yourself a drink! Make sure you have a tool handy to crack open a beer or pour a glass of wine. You deserve it. Will probably be the best $10 spent on any of these 20 items, though there's a high probability that if you were drinking beer and wine in college, you may already own this item. Look at that; you just saved $10.

Also, if you want to save even more money, not all of these items need to be purchased new, and certainly not all from Amazon. Depending on the item and your level of comfort on buying "used" versions, you can find a lot of these items at garage sales, consignment shops, and discount retailers. Often you'll see "for sale" items advertised in neighborhood groups on various social media platforms. You may be lucky enough to come across someone who, just a few years before you, graduated and set up their own "first kitchen," and perhaps adding some gently-used items to your kitchen will help you offset the overall out-of-pocket expenses required to get your kitchen fully set up and ready to go!

Are there other things you can use to beef up your kitchen? Of course there are. I would recommend starting here and then adding as you need. Most recipes can be cooked using only the items mentioned above. Of course, you'll also need to grab dishes, silverware, and glassware to use while eating all of those yummy home-cooked meals you'll be making. Set yourself up for success; if your kitchen has all you'll need to make a meal at home, you're more likely to use it. And if you can get great at meal planning and prepping and keeping a budget in mind, you're likely to save money and stay healthy in the process.

GYM MEMBERSHIPS/FITNESS OPTIONS

Most colleges now offer pretty badass facilities where you can get a great workout in, take a spin or HIIT class, jump in a pool for some laps or run miles and miles on one of their 100 treadmills. Oh, and it's FREE (well, not exactly free, as it's bundled up into your overall college tuition). But still, the average college fitness center rivals some of the best gyms offered in cities around the country. I wish I recognized how amazing it was to have access to a state-of-the-art facility like the one I had in college. After graduating and moving to New York City, I spent more than $100 a month for a gym that wasn't even half as good as what I had in college for free!

A lot of people want to belong to the "fancy" gym, and if that's your thing, then go for it. You totally can. Remember, you're an adult now and can spend your money however you want! But before committing to a long-term contract, ask yourself WHY you are going to the gym. Are you going there for the social scene, or are you going there to work out? Do you put makeup on before you go because you know you'll end up seeing people you know, or do you throw on whatever is clean and get to work?

There's no right answer, but I want you to understand your why and make sure that your actions—including those in the dietary realm—are in line with that. For example, you may spend $100 on a gym membership and even some extra money for personal training sessions or a boutique spin class but then crush late-night pizza four times a week. If your goal is to stay in shape, lose weight, or build muscle, yet your overall habits don't support that, then is the gym membership even worth it? That $100 could be a great investment if reallocated somewhere else.

CHEAPER EXERCISE OPTIONS

1. **Fitness center on campus:** If you live nearby the college you attended, sometimes you're able to access the facility that the students use. Check with them to see if there's any sort of discounted alumni rate available.

2. **Fitness center in your apartment:** Many of the newer apartment complexes offer a fitness center right in the apartment building. Not having to step foot outside to go the gym is a great option, especially on those rainy or cold days when your motivation to work out may be lower than normal. In almost all cases, access to these facilities is free for tenants, so this option would be a massive money saver.

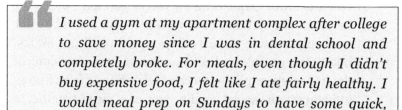

> *I used a gym at my apartment complex after college to save money since I was in dental school and completely broke. For meals, even though I didn't buy expensive food, I felt like I ate fairly healthy. I would meal prep on Sundays to have some quick, easy meals ready to go for the week."*
>
> - Preston, University of Texas at Austin, Class of 2009

3. **Online options:** As you know, there is a wealth of information available online, and the world of health and fitness is no different. Searching YouTube or the app store for workouts will reveal a ton of free and nearly-free options. There are many free apps that give you basics or, for a few dollars a month, will provide you with full workout programs. Companies such as Beachbody offer libraries of thousands of workouts with top trainers for $100/year, and there's no need to leave your house to get a great workout in. Just stream from your phone, tablet, laptop, or Smart TV, and you're fully equipped with a great plan to get results. And for $8-ish a month, you can't beat it.

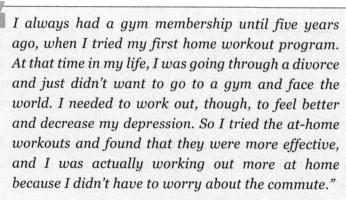

> *I always had a gym membership until five years ago, when I tried my first home workout program. At that time in my life, I was going through a divorce and just didn't want to go to a gym and face the world. I needed to work out, though, to feel better and decrease my depression. So I tried the at-home workouts and found that they were more effective, and I was actually working out more at home because I didn't have to worry about the commute."*
>
> - Allison, University of Florida, Class of 1996

4. **Get outside:** Depending on where you live—and your tolerance for wet and cold weather—you can take your workouts outside almost all year round. Runs, walks, hikes... get outside and get your sweat on! Using some of the free workout plans you can find online or from fitness influencers on social media, you can piece together a great outdoor workout, involving no equipment, which will get help you hit your fitness goals for the wonderful price of $0/month.

TRAVEL POST-COLLEGE

Once you leave college, you'll find that your friends start to spread out across the country and, in some cases, across the world! No longer can you make one call and have your closest friends come cry with you for an episode of your favorite show or meet you at the bar to catch the game. They may have moved back to their hometown or a city completely across the country from where you settled.

The great news (or maybe not-so-great news depending on how you look at it) is that technology keeps us closer than ever. Between FaceTime/Skype/WhatsApp and other virtual videoconference tools, you can "see" your friends and family whenever you want. But nothing replaces the in-person companionship that you lose upon graduation. My college friends and I talk about this all the time. We joke about moving to a big compound with our families (if they'll come!) and how we took for granted all the time we had when we were no more than across the hall or campus from one another for those four glorious years.

So you'll want to see them—and you should—but when it comes to doing so on a budget, there are a few things to keep in mind:

1. **How much time do you get off from work?** You'll likely have some vacation/PTO (Paid Time Off) benefits that come with being a full-time employee. But one thing

to keep in mind: just because you have the time doesn't mean you're able to take it exactly when you want to. Your company could have a "blackout period" during an especially busy season where no scheduled vacations are allowed. Also, vacation time is often earned. You don't start on day one with two weeks of vacation that's ready to be used. It may take the entire first year to earn those two weeks. Perhaps you are lucky enough to work for a company with an unlimited vacation schedule. That's awesome, but you need to be mindful of when you're taking this vacation. How's your performance been? What will your boss think if you take the time off? Would she say, "Great, enjoy, you deserve it!" Or would the feeling be, "He's going away *again*?" Having good awareness of your performance and what's going on in the company will help you manage your time off better. Also, alerting your manager about your planned time off before you book anything always goes a long way. Coming to your manager and letting her know that you've booked a trip for the following month, before officially receiving the permission to take off, isn't a good look. Also, the more notice you give, the better. Approaching your manager and letting her know that you'd like to visit family or take a trip this summer but before booking, you wanted to find a time that would work for the team. That will go a long way.

2. How much money do you have to spend on travel?
Unless you've planned ahead, most people don't include a travel budget in their monthly expense planning, so in addition to all of the other costs necessary to keep you going (car, gas, insurance, rent, utilities, food and entertainment, etc.), your bank account may be shocked when it suddenly sees flights and hotels booked. Or you could take my early-20s approach: throw it all on a credit card and pretend it didn't happen (more to come on that). If you know you'll travel throughout the year, then start saving now. Take some money each week to put in

a travel fund, and then empty that shit out by visiting everyone or everywhere you can!

3. **Travel during the off-season or on "off days" if possible.** Just as you liked to take advantage of Spring Break in college, so do many families. In March or April, most schools shut down for up to a week, and the airlines know it (and charge accordingly). Avoiding travel during these months will help keep travel expenses down. Memorial Day, Fourth of July, and Labor Day are popular times to travel as well because many people can sneak in a longer weekend without taking time off of work (assuming your company is closed in recognition of those holidays). Other major holidays where you can see a spike in prices include Christmas and New Year's, but flying on the Wednesday before and Sunday after Thanksgiving will be the most bank-breaking. Those two days are the most expensive travel days of the year. Outside of major holidays, flying on Tuesdays and Wednesdays will likely reduce your airfare, but if those two days aren't available, opt for a Thursday or Saturday next. Sundays, Mondays, and Fridays will cost you a bit more. Having said all of this, sometimes there's nothing you can do. Perhaps you can't take more than one day off of work, or you are the best man in a wedding over Labor Day. Maybe your mom is counting on you to come home for the holidays. You've got to go. But, when given the option, keep these tips in mind.

4. **Can you see more than one friend at a time or plan annual trips?** My girlfriends and I have a standing May weekend where we all try to get together. It's not perfect: life gets in the way for some of us some of the years, but out of the 10 of us, usually we can get seven or eight of us together, which is (a) a nice way to avoid multiple trips and time off to see them individually and (b) way more fun getting together as a group!

And forget all of the friend travel. What if you just want to get away by yourself for a little R&R? Taking time away from your work and day-to-day responsibilities is important. Recharging your batteries and coming back refreshed, and perhaps a little tan, is never a bad thing. Be smart about when and where you travel, and you should be able to sneak away a few times of the year and still hit your professional and financial goals.

After college, you'll be making more money than you ever have, and if you aren't careful, you'll notice that money goes out as quickly as it comes in. With the right approach toward budgeting and money management, you should be able to "do it all." You'll be able to enjoy time out with friends, take trips with those you care most about, and enjoy other non-work activities. You'll be able to feed and clothe yourself and even start building a little bit of savings. But it doesn't come without focused effort. You've got this!

Key takeaways:

1. MEAL PLANNING AND SMART SHOPPING CAN HELP REDUCE YOUR MONTHLY FOOD BILL, ONE OF THE LARGEST VARIABLE COSTS YOU'LL HAVE EACH MONTH. INVEST IN SOME ESSENTIAL KITCHEN ITEMS SO YOU'RE ABLE TO COOK MORE AT HOME AND REDUCE YOUR DINING-OUT EXPENSES.

2. WHEN IT COMES TO SELECTING A GYM OR FITNESS STUDIO, MAKE SURE YOU'RE AWARE OF THE MONTHLY COSTS AND FACTOR THAT INTO YOUR BUDGET. DON'T FORGET LESS EXPENSIVE OPTIONS IF YOU'RE FINDING THAT YOUR MONTHLY EXPENSES ARE GETTING A LITTLE TOO HIGH.

3. SAVE MONEY ON TRAVEL BY PLANNING AHEAD, FLYING AT OFF-PEAK TIMES, AND SEEING MULTIPLE FRIENDS AT ONCE.

Chapter Eight

HOW DO I STAY OUT OF (OR GET OUT OF) CREDIT CARD DEBT?

You know how sometimes you know a lot about something because you have a degree in that subject or have done loads of research in that area? And other times your experience comes from living through a real-life situation, one where you may have made the wrong decisions and learned the "hard way?" Well, let's just say that I've got the scars to prove that my experience with credit cards and debt came from The School of Hard Knocks. I was in deep credit card debt in the years following college and am proud to say that I no longer have that problem. I know exactly how to get into debt and also know exactly how to get out of it—and stay out.

Disclaimer: If you are currently in serious debt and feeling underwater, please work with a professional who can help you formulate a plan to get out of it.

If you are not in debt or carry a small balance on your cards, I believe that you can get some good ideas from this chapter. As you know, I'm not a credit counselor, but this book would be incomplete without sharing at least some high-level info about the basics of credit cards.

The minute you turn 18, you'll start getting solicitations for credit cards. And they'll keep coming, possibly until the end of time. If you don't have your own credit card already, you need one. Having credit is important. When you apply for an apartment or buy a car or a home, your creditworthiness will determine if you get approved and the interest rate that you receive. If you have bad credit, that's no bueno. If you have "no credit," that's tough too because lenders or landlords have no history to reference to see if you manage your credit responsibly, so they're unsure of the risk level when partnering with you. Ultimately, this will cost you, in either missed opportunities or in cold, hard cash. Applying for a car loan with a lack of credit history or bad credit will get you a higher interest rate and often a higher monthly payment (if you're not denied altogether). Fair or not, you'll end up paying much more for that car than someone with a solid credit history.

So how do you build that history? Well, the first step is to apply for some cards. But before signing up for the first offer you see, take time to do some research. It's critical that you shop around for cards that match your lifestyle and offer a rate that will make sense for you over time. Often, cards with low introductory rates come with an annual fee, and eventually that low rate will morph into a higher one.

If you already have a card that you're happy with, when is the last time you called the credit card company to ask if it's possible to lower your APR (annual percentage rate) or increase your line of credit (which is a good indicator of creditworthiness)? Maybe they have a new offer that you're unaware of. I like to let them know that I'm thinking of consolidating cards and that I'd be closing my account if there's nothing they can do to make it more attractive to retain me as a customer. More often than not, they'll find a way to make it happen in the hopes that you'll remain a cardholder of theirs.

UNDERSTANDING ALL OF THE NUMBERS/TERMS ASSOCIATED WITH CREDIT CARDS

This may make your head spin, but in order to make sound financial decisions, you need to be educated on some of the terminology associated with credit cards.

APR/Interest Rate: Cards will come with either a fixed interest rate or a variable interest rate. You need to determine whether a low, fixed-rate card is better for you than one that offers a zero percent introductory rate (and other perks like miles or points). The fixed rates can change as overall interest rates increase, but they need to notify you in writing and provide you with fifteen days' notice. The notification will come in one of those envelopes you probably throw away automatically, so before doing so, always take a look to see what it entails. Most people miss these changes and suddenly wonder why it's taken so long to pay off that bar tab from their buddy's bachelor party. A variable-rate card is just that: it's variable and can change at any time and without notice. Additionally, the rate can double or triple if you miss a payment, so again, take a look at what you're signing up for.

Minimum Payment: This is the minimum monthly payment amount needed to remain in good standing and avoid any late fees. This is what the credit card wants you to pay, not necessarily what you *should* pay. It means that all of the rest of the money that you haven't paid will be charged interest. The card company is hoping you only pay the minimum. That means they can still make money off of the balance on the card. For example, if you have a $250 balance and pay the minimum payment of $20, you'll be paying interest on the $230 that went unpaid.

Late Fee: What happens when you make your payment a few days late? Is there a grace period? Often, the late fee ranges from $25-$40, though if it's your first "offense" they may waive it. I've asked them to waive it a second time and they politely told me to take a hike, so know that this "beg for forgiveness" strategy isn't one that can be used over and over again. Moral of the story: pay your bills on time, even if you can't pay all of it.

Balance Transfer Fee: In order to tempt you to increase the balance on your card, credit card companies will allow you to transform your balance from another card (with a higher interest rate) to their card with a lower interest rate. This is a temporary rate, and there's a fee associated with it. You can expect it to be either around 3 percent of the balance or a fixed minimum amount. For example, it may cost you $90 to transfer $3,000, but if you can pay off that $3k over 12 months at zero percent interest, then the $90 was worth spending. (Side note: this tactic helped me when I was paying off my debt, but more on that later.)

Annual Fee: Credit cards with lots of perks and rewards often come with annual fees. The fee may be waived for the first year, but in the second year—and beyond—you can expect that fee to be tacked on to your balance. These fees can range from $50 to $400 for some of the most "rewarding" cards out there. My mother pays almost $500 a year for a credit card with high perks, but she takes full advantage and ends up saving money by using that card. To her, it's worth it. You need to ask yourself if the fee you'll be paying is worth it for you.

Payment Date: When is your payment due? Can you change this? Sometimes you can ask for a different date. For example, if all of your other bills are due on the 1st of the month, perhaps you can pay your card on the 15th to space your monthly payments out a bit. It's worth a call to find out!

Over-the-Limit Fee: What happens if you overspend? When you're first starting to establish credit, you may notice that your credit limit will be low, maybe between $500 and $1000. What happens if you have a $750 limit and you have already have a $600 balance, need to stock up on food, do a big grocery store run, and spend $175? The credit card company may allow that sale to go through, but you're technically over the limit. What happens then? Make sure you understand that fully, as all cards are different.

Cash Advance Rate: I don't even want to explain this, because it's something you should not use unless you are in a complete emergency and have no other access to cash that second. However, it is an option on all cards, so it's worth understanding. Essentially, it means that you are borrowing money from your credit card. Keep in mind that you will be forced to pay a higher amount back, due to the lofty fee that is associated with that transaction.

Every card is slightly different, and card issuers may offer additional options. Some are valuable and save you money. Some aren't and don't. Some might be added automatically and give you no choice. Some you might have to ask for. Some you might be able to turn down. Some you might agree to without knowing it if you don't read all the fine print on your monthly statement.

Lastly, don't be fooled by the fancy "pre-approved" label on the outside of the credit card invitation envelope. All that means is that the card company is familiar with your credit history and credit standing. There's no guarantee you'll get any special rate when it comes to the terms of the deal. And, after you apply, you may find that you aren't approved for the initial deal, which may have been what attracted you in the first place.

RESPONSIBLE CREDIT CARD USE

Congratulations! You've got a credit card or two. That's step one. Step two is using it responsibly and staying out of debt.

How do you do that, you ask? Well, it's pretty simple. Don't spend more than you currently have in your checking account, and pay your full bill on time every month. Cool? All right, great—no need to explain any further. That's how you stay out of debt. Seems pretty simple, right? Well, just because it's simple doesn't mean it's easy.

For those of you who don't have much of a credit history, you need to start using the cards you do have. Find opportunities where you would normally use cash or your debit card and use your credit card instead. Pay for a small purchase at CVS with your card and then immediately pay it off. Then do it again a few days later. And then again a few days later. These small purchases and on-time payments will start creating the history you're currently lacking. Additionally, as you start to make bigger purchases like appliances, furniture or electronics, take advantage of the store's financing options and be sure to pay on time. This will also add to a positive credit history.

There are so many things you don't *have* to spend money on but that you *want* to spend money on! Happy hours. Birthday parties. Brunches, lunches, dinners out with friends. Taking cabs or Ubers instead of walking. Travel. Clothes. Fun. Life! Please don't mistake this chapter for one that's telling you to ignore all of the stuff that makes life worth living. Some of my best memories were made on various trips with friends and family and all of those alcohol-fueled celebrations (from what I can remember!) for all the birthdays I've had since I turned twenty-one. Plus, you need something cute to wear to all of those events, right? Of course!

Here's the deal: I'm just asking you to be aware of what you truly need, and separate what you *need* from what you *want*. Once you know what you need and have covered that, you can use whatever money is left to focus on what you want. And there may be choices involved. Instead of three trips to the bar this week, you may need to settle for one. Instead of dinner out and a boozy brunch on the same weekend, why don't you pick one? Or offer to cook in instead. Don't become a hermit, but be responsible and remember that every dollar you spend today could be worth $5 down the line. We will talk about this more later in the chapter when we dive into the Compound Effect.

When I moved out on my own (after sharing an apartment with four people), I had no concept of a budget because I'd never needed one before. As a result, I quickly maxed out my credit cards. Just because you have good credit and a high limit on your cards doesn't mean you should aim to reach that limit. My family bailed me out, and mint.com helped me categorize my finances, find wasteful spending, and organize a budget."

- Nikki, James Madison University, Class of 2005

Right after college, I lived on credit cards, but I was really good about timely payments so I had very good credit... at least, until my boyfriend at the time moved out. I suddenly had to pay all the bills by myself, and I was at a commission-based job. To make matters worse, all of my friends and I had to rely on payday loans to make it from week to week. I was robbing Peter to pay Paul (Peter being my credit card bills and Paul being my food/gas/rent/ car payment). It was a vicious cycle that took years to get out of. If I had only used my credit card for emergencies or paid the balance completely each month, I would have been in much better shape."

- Portia, Florida Atlantic University, Class of 2002

> *Ugh, credit card debt. For me, it started when I financed law school with loans. I didn't need as much as I took out, but I took the money anyway and led a very extravagant life for a student on loans. This translated into credit card debt when I started working as a lawyer. I recall specifically leaving my firm one lunch break and heading to Saks, which was right next door. I had my eye on a Gucci hat. Who the hell needs a Gucci hat? I bought a bag instead. But who buys a Gucci bag on credit and then pays the minimum credit card payment? It was not good. I was never great at budgeting. Thank God for family support."*
>
> - Alyse, University of Florida, Class of 1998

CREDIT CARD DEBT

I hope that you, as the reader, don't know anything about debt. Hopefully you got a full ride to a great school, manage your money so well that you only spend what you have, and pay any credit cards you have in full each month. If this description doesn't describe you, let's talk a little more about debt.

According to a *Money Magazine* article from August of 2018, Gen Z and younger millennials (ages 18-24) averaged $22,000 worth of debt. Student loans accounted for 28 percent of that total, and credit card balances made up the next largest portion of that number. It makes sense that student loans would make up the majority of this amount. In fact, experts actually consider student loans to be "good debt," as they generally come with lower interest rates and, in some cases, come with tax advantages. Now, if you ask most people with outstanding loans, they wouldn't say their student debt is a good thing. But if a creditor is looking at your account and sees $20,000 in student loans, they don't view it in the same way as $20,000 on credit cards.

I balled up a good amount of credit card debt and had a not-so-fantastic credit score while in college and newly married. I paid off my debt, closed the accounts, and am now just an authorized user on my husband's credit cards. Because of this, I had to see a credit counselor in order to apply for an FHA loan for our current house when we first purchased it."

- Kelly, West Chester University, Class of 2004

Once you jump into the "older millennial" category (ages 25 to 34), that balance almost doubles, rising to $42,000. Things have shifted a bit by then; the largest portion of that balance now is credit card debt, around 25 percent, and student debt only accounts for 16 percent. As you grow older, although your salary is hopefully going up, so are your expenses. Often, your disposable income is starting to shrink, while additional pressures on your wallet increase.

I grew up being taught financial responsibility, and then I got married. My ex-husband was not afraid of credit card debt and felt that 'he made good money' so that we could afford it. Well, we never followed a budget! We just spent, spent, spent. Don't get me wrong, that was fun, but wow, it was so suffocating. When we got divorced, we had $51K in credit card debt and nothing to show for it! After the divorce, I was able to use my knowledge as a Registered Dietitian to start a side business to help tackle that debt and the attorney fees from the divorce. I am proud to say that with hard work, I am almost debt-free five years later! My biggest advice is to stick to a budget and make your money work for you. It is so freeing to not be a slave to credit cards."

- Allison, University of Florida, Class of 1996

My story? Well, after school I got a job that was commission-based. I tried my hand at entrepreneurship and didn't manage my money well. Because my income varied week by week, it was hard to budget, and any money in my checking account went right to rent. I also had to eat, pay utilities, put gas in my car, insure that car and my health, and furnish my overpriced San Diego apartment.

I was spending above my means, and I didn't want to stop. At the time, it felt like a dirty secret; I didn't want to decline an invite for a night out or drinks with my friends because I "couldn't afford it." So I went. If my boyfriend and I wanted take-out, even though we had food in the fridge, we got it. I put that baby right on my credit card. Oh, and the rotting groceries in the fridge? Yeah, I put those on my credit card too.

Clothing? Yeah, I needed more of that constantly. And I tricked myself into thinking it wasn't a big deal; after all, I was shopping at Marshall's and T.J. Maxx, not super fancy stores. But a few $100 trips to "discount" stores add up each month, and when my bill came in, I saw two numbers: total balance and minimum payment due. That minimum felt a lot better than the actual balance. So instead of paying the $350 total balance, I'd pay $50 and promise myself that I would pay the total amount the following month. But the balance wasn't $300 the following month; it was $300 PLUS the high interest I'd accumulated since the last bill. Oh, and I had to eat, shop, and go out over the course of that month too. Now, the initial $300, plus the interest, plus the new purchases, turned into a new balance of $650. This time I'd pay $100, and this would go on and on and on. And this wasn't my only card. I had multiple cards, and each time I got close to the maximum limit, the card companies were "nice" enough to raise my credit limit. I was making on-time payments, so my credit score was actually in good shape. The companies were tracking my habits, knowing that it was highly likely that if I had a higher limit, I'd spend more. They were right. Limits went up. So did balances.

Over time, it all added up, and by the time I was twenty-five, my debt peaked at almost $30,000 in credit card balances. Thirty thousand dollars—holy shit! I couldn't believe I had arrived here. I was embarrassed, ashamed at how I had mismanaged everything so poorly. On the surface, all looked good, but each week I'd be crunching numbers and trying my best to figure out ways to work my cards against each other to lower rates, switch my due dates, and increase my limit in order to help increase my credit score.

I had to look at my habits with money. I'd been spending with reckless abandon, making impulse choices, and never saying no to a want. I had to do a complete overhaul on my day-to-day spending and really look at some of the habits that were negatively affecting me.

1. **Dining out/take-out:** Sure, it's less expensive to cook at home, but you know what's easier? Take-out. Or eating in the restaurants. Plus, I hate cooking, so it was always a preferred option for me. Packing your lunch for work? You could, but that's definitely not as fun as going out with coworkers mid-day. Want a coffee? Well, the free coffee in the break room is okay, but there's a Starbucks a block away, and it's tastier to just grab a quick Grande of whatever the featured drink is. When it came to dinner, take-out just made so much sense. Living in New York City (and now anywhere else with apps like Door Dash, Uber Eats, etc.), you could literally get anything you wanted delivered to your door in under thirty minutes. And who wants to cook after a long day at work anyway? Not this girl, I'll tell you that much. But you know what I wanted more than avoiding cooking? Getting out of this suffocating mound of debt.

2. **Entertainment:** I was going out a lot, paying for overpriced cocktails and beers usually three or four times a week. A quick happy hour or dinner and drinks with friends is harmless, right? Well, tally them up over weeks and months, and they add up fast. I don't recommend

cutting this out completely, but start to look at your own habits around eating/drinking out. Could you cut back a bit? Could you go out once on the weekend instead of both nights? Could you skip the happy hour or commit to having one drink, and that's it, before headed home? It's better for your health and your wallet. It seems like a win-win to me! Could you host a get-together or meet at someone else's house instead of going out somewhere? Maybe you could all cook together and serve your own drinks, avoiding the expense of getting there and back, along with paying for the dinner, drinks, tax, and tip. You're really getting together to spend time with friends; that can be done at home!

3. **Travel:** The hope is that you will meet many new local friends throughout your first few years after college. And they may be friends you have for life! But you just spent four years with some incredible people, and not seeing them daily sucks. So here come the weekend trips. Chances are your friends from college have spread across the country, so getting to them often requires some planning. When I was in California, I'd head to the East Coast a lot, and then when I lived in NYC, the trips would be out west. In 2009, when I was 27, I'm pretty sure my entire annual salary went to weddings and wedding-related activity. I'm from Pennsylvania, and my husband's from California. We both grew up hours away from where we went to college and ended up settling in a different part of the country completely. This meant that we had friends located all over the United States who all decided to fall in love and tie the knot at the same time. In one calendar year, we had fifteen weddings (including ours!), and ten of them involved a flight to get there. And not only a flight—let's not forget lodging, entertainment while there, the wedding gift, and if you're in the wedding, forget saving money. Being in the wedding party means wedding showers and bachelorette/bachelor parties and tuxedos and bridesmaid dresses galore. We went to all

fifteen and even split up for two since they were on the same weekend. We don't regret being at any of these weddings, but we also didn't budget properly for them. They all went on our credit cards because, of course, how could we *not* be there?

4. **Shopping:** Keeping up with the latest fashions costs money. Again, I wasn't shopping at crazy high-end stores, but I wanted nice things. Shoes, bags, a new "going-out outfit," and, of course, tons of dresses for all of those weddings! Can't be seen in the same thing twice, right? Looking back on my closet full of clothes is sickening. My mom still gives me shit when she sees something that's been hanging in my closet for a year and still has a price tag on it. Doesn't matter if the amount on the tag is $10 or $100; it's the principle. I get it. And I regret it.

Does any of this resonate with you? Do you find that some of these coffees here, Target runs there, happy hours with friends and coworkers, or weekend trips start adding up? If you answered yes to these questions, please know that I am not suggesting you stop cold turkey. I think it's critically important to get to know your coworkers outside of the office, have a social life both locally and out of town, and stay clothed and caffeinated. But if you can scale back, even by a small amount, those smaller changes will add up.

HOW TO DETERMINE IF YOUR SPENDING IS ON POINT

Take a look at your last three months of spending. Go ahead. I'll wait. If you use cash a lot, this will be more difficult, but if you use a debit or credit card, this shouldn't be too hard to track. Literally go line by line on your last three statements and see where your money is going. What did you find? For example, let's say you spent $60 on Starbucks in one month; can you cut it to $30, going once a week instead of two times a week? Can you avoid that extra trip to Target or stick to what is on your list, resisting all the cute stuff you see while wandering the aisles? Perhaps the new drive-up option is good for you. You show up, get only what you need, and don't even see the impulse purchases that often tempt you once you're inside the store. Take a look also at how many times you dined out. How much are you spending on groceries, and how often are you tossing food that's gone bad because decided you suddenly weren't in the mood for the meal you'd planned for that night? You may find that you can make small changes that will lead to a better handle on your money, without totally missing out on the things you like to do. I bet you could find $100 - $200 in your monthly discretionary spending that you could re-allocate to savings or use to pay off of your existing debt.

I wish I budgeted for everyday better. I wish I was more mindful of what I spent and really evaluated if what I was choosing to spend my money on was worth it. Just because the money was there doesn't mean it needed to be spent. Did I really need to eat out every day? Did I need a new outfit for every presentation or night out? Lattes every afternoon? No! The more I made, the more I spent, and it wasn't necessary. Luckily, doing the big things right helped me stay on track, but now that I am out of those habits I realize how unnecessary the day-to-day spending was."

- Justin, Syracuse, Class of 2006

PAYING OFF DEBT

There are two main methods of tackling your credit card debt, and if you do enough Google searches, you'll find tons of articles lauding one to be better than the other. Either way, if you've got debt, create a plan and start paying it off today. Don't wait until you make more money; get the habit going immediately.

The first technique, which has been popularized by Dave Ramsey, is called the "snowball method." This approach suggests that you prioritize your smallest debts first, regardless of the interest rate. Start by listing out all of your debts from smallest to largest, and then pay the minimum balance (I'd suggest adding $1 to the minimum, but more on that later) on each debt except for the one with the smallest amount. Take any extra money you have and pay as much as you can to the card with the smallest balance. Do that over and over again until it's paid off. Once that card is paid off, take the money you were paying toward that first card and use it to help knock out the next card. Rinse and repeat until all debts are paid off. The theory here is that you'll start to feel the momentum in seeing the debts, even the small ones, disappear. This momentum will motivate you to continue this habit, and because of that, you've got a better chance of paying the debt off completely. It's similar to going on a diet; if you start to see some results in the first week, there's a higher likelihood that you'll stick with the diet week over week. Ramsey explains this in greater detail in his book *The Total Money Makeover*. I suggest you pick up a copy. It's a great read.

Before you start tackling the debt, Ramsey recommends saving $1,000 in an "emergency fund." Once that fund is established, do not touch it unless, you guessed it, an emergency arises. Then be sure that all bills are up-to-date. They don't need to be paid off, but they need to be current without an outstanding payment. Once the emergency fund has reached $1,000 and all bills are in good standing, then start to implement the snowball method.

An Example of the Debt Snowball:

	BALANCE	MINIMUM MONTHLY PAYMENT
Medical Bill	$480	$45
Credit Card Bill	$2,100	$78
Car Loan	$9,000	$135
Student Loan	$50,000	$196

Take a look at the image above and pretend all of the debt on the chart is yours. Using the snowball method, you would make minimum payments on everything except the medical bill. Let's say you have an extra $200 each month because you tracked your spending, decided to cut out some of the trips to the bar, and dropped from five lattes a week to three.

Since you're adding that newfound $200 to your debt and paying $245 this month on the medical bill, that balance will be down to $235. Next month, you pay that $235 completely, and suddenly that bill is gone. Cross it off of your list. Then, you can take the freed-up $245 you had allocated to the medical bill and attack the credit card debt, paying a total of $323 ($245 plus the $78 minimum payment). In about six months, you'll wave goodbye to that credit card. It's now paid off too, assuming you were disciplined and didn't purchase more on that card.

So, now your medical bill is gone. The credit card debt is wiped out. Add the $323 that you've been putting toward the credit card payments to the $135 payment you've been making monthly toward your car. Paying $458 toward your car each month will quickly chip away at that $9,000. You'll own the car and no longer have a payment; how nice is that!

By the time you reach the student loan—which is your largest debt—you can put $654 a month toward it. Nice work!

A DIFFERENT APPROACH

Suze Orman, another financial guru, wants you to take a similar approach, but she wants you to pay down the cards with the highest interest rates first. This means that if you have a $900 credit card bill with a 23 percent interest rate, you should knock that out before focusing on a $1,000 bill with 12 percent interest. Mathematically, it makes the most sense, and you'll maximize your money this way. She talks all about this strategy in a great book called *Young, Broke and Fabulous*. This is the approach I took, and in about 18 months, I was completely debt-free, and I cannot tell you the relief I felt once I made that last payment!

UNDERSTANDING YOUR CREDIT SCORE

There are a few numbers that people may be embarrassed to share with others. Some that come to mind are age, income level, weight, and credit score: all VERY personal information that most people don't want to share with the general public. Whether you have a "good" score or "bad" one, you need to know what it represents and that it's an important data point that future lenders consider when deciding to loan you money, finance a car loan, provide you with a line of credit, and help you buy your first home. Even if you're not in the market for any of these things right now, someday you may be, and the habits you have toward money now will either positively or negatively affect your future score and financial health.

WHAT DOES YOUR CREDIT SCORE CONSIST OF?

According to Equifax, here's the breakdown of your credit score:

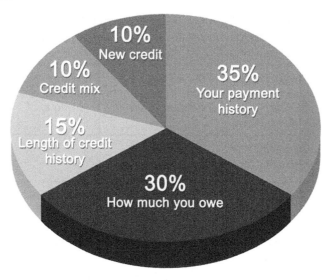

Payment history: 35 percent. Listen. Pay your shit on time. It's as simple as that. A late payment of thirty days or more will stay on your account for up to seven years. SEVEN!

Isn't that crazy? Well, although it may be crazy, it's also true. So use a calendar, set a reminder in your phone, put post-its all over your house. Whatever it takes, pay your cards on time. Even if you can't pay the full balance, pay at least a dollar over the minimum payment, and pay it on time. Almost every card can be enrolled in automatic payments. This means it's linked to your checking account so even if you forget, the technology won't. According to FICO, past long-term behavior is used to forecast future long-term behavior. Make sure the creditors see consistent, timely payments when they look back on your past behavior. This is the *most* important factor in calculating credit scores; do not mess this up.

Now let's talk about making the "minimum" payment each month. A few years ago, credit card companies started including a "payoff calendar" with each statement. If you get electronic statements, you may not pay attention to this. Hell, if you get paper statements, you may not notice this either. It looks something like this.

Minimum Payment Warning: If you make only the minimum payment each period, you will pay more in interest and it will take you longer to pay off your balance. For example:

If you make no additional charges using this card and each month you pay...	You will pay off the balance shown on this statement in about...	And you will end up paying an estimated total of...
Only the minimum payment	8 years	$3,735
$73	3 years	$2,641 (Savings=$1,094)

If you would like information about credit counseling services, call 1-866-797-2885.

You'll notice that if you pay the minimum only (which is around $30 in this case), it will take you eight years to pay it off. If you pay $73, an amount they suggest, you'll pay it off five years sooner and save $1,094 in the process.

So, why pay a dollar more than the minimum? On your credit report, the lender is able to mark one of two boxes: "minimum payment made" or "more than the minimum payment made." If you have a consistent history of paying just the minimum, it may appear that you're financially stretched thin, which is not an appealing quality when evaluating someone's creditworthiness. If the minimum payment required is $25 and you can't pay the full balance, pay $26. The extra dollar will bring you to the "more than the minimum payment made" box, and that will fare better for you in the long run.

Speaking of credit, you should also be reviewing your credit report often. As a U.S. Citizen, you are entitled to three free credit reports per year, one from each of the three major credit reporting agencies (Experian, Equifax, and TransUnion). If you haven't taken advantage of the free credit report you're entitled to, head to www.freecreditreport.com and check it out. This particular site does not require the credit card to get your report as some others do. If you are up for spending a little money, you're able to opt for a more detailed report that includes your credit scores according to each of these companies. You may find that your credit score is best with one particular agency. For example, let's say your score is 710 with TransUnion and 690 with both Equifax and Experian. If the lender that you're working with uses TransUnion to check your credit, you may end up with better terms due to that higher score.

Check out the Appendix in the back of the book for a sample credit report.

Debt-to-Credit Ratio: 30 percent. This involves how much debt you have compared to how much available credit you have. For example, let's say you have a $500 balance on a card with a limit of $750 and an $800 balance on a card with a $1,000 limit. Assuming you have no other credit card debt, that means that you have $1,300 in total due out of a possible $1,750 available. That is a high "debt-to-credit ratio." You are slightly more than 74 percent "maxed out," and that is considered high when someone is looking at your credit. Statistically speaking, it is likely that you'll max out completely, and because of that, you may appear to be a risky option to lend to. It'd be better if that same $1,300 were spread over cards that totaled $4,000 in available credit. Then you'd only be approaching 33 percent of your maximum borrowing limit.

When I was trying to pay off my mountain of debt and repair my credit score, I was told to call my credit cards and ask them to RAISE my limit. I know, I know; that sounds crazy. More chances for me to get deeper in debt. That's what the credit card companies thought too. That's why they all said YES! They were hoping that I'd go into more debt. That would mean they'd make more on interest, late fees, etc. (Please note: I only recommend doing this if you feel confident you can be disciplined in your plan to pay off your debt and not be tempted by the additional spending power you just received.) In the example above, if the person with the $1,300 limit across both cards asked the credit card companies to raise his limit by $1,000 each, he'd now have $1,300 in debt but an overall limit of $3,800. Overnight, he'd go from a 74 percent debt-to-credit ratio down to a 34 percent debt-to-credit ratio. Suddenly, he looks like he's got a handle on managing his debt. Then, as he chips away at that $1,300, the debt-to-credit ratio starts looking more and more favorable, and eventually, he will start getting letters in the mail saying that his limit was raised even further. FICO views borrowers with a high credit utilization as people who are not handling their debt responsibly, so take a look at yours and, if you are approaching your limits, set a plan to get that under control. If you're looking for a benchmark, FICO says that the people with the best credit have less than six percent credit utilization with no more than three cards carrying balances and less than $3,000 in total balance (from Creditcards.com article).

Since paying off my debt and then opening other cards, I now have close to $80,000 in available credit on my cards. One card alone has a $40,000 credit line; this is all due to my history with the card company and the health in which I keep the account. I hope never to need to put $40k on my cards for anything, but knowing it's there, if I'm ever in a jam, is so comforting. Plus, other lenders that run my credit see my high creditworthiness, which has led to better rates on car and home loans, saving me money each month and overall over the course of the entire loan.

Length of Credit History: 15 percent. This is just what it sounds like. This part of your overall rating captures how long each account has been open as well as how long it's been since the account's most recent action. A longer credit history, as discussed earlier, gives lenders a better snapshot of your past behavior, and having long-standing positive relationships with lenders will help your score. If you already have good credit history, don't close an account you've had for years, even if it's at a zero balance. Having a decade-long relationship with AMEX is sexy to a lender!

New Credit and Credit Mix: 10 percent each. Opening too many credit lines at the same time may suggest that you are in some financial trouble and that you need substantial access to a large amount of credit. FICO recommends applying for and opening new accounts as needed. New accounts will lower your overall average account age, and that has a larger effect on your score, especially if you don't have a lot of other credit information.

Credit mix is a hard category to explain because it's sometimes hard to control the mix of debt you have. What if you didn't need to take out school loans? What if you are able to pay for a car in full upfront and don't need a car payment? What if you use mostly cash for your purchases? Experts say the proven ability to repay a variety of debt products indicates that the borrower can handle all sorts of credit and is generally viewed as less risky for lenders. This is why people who have no credit cards tend to be viewed as higher risk than people who have managed credit cards responsibly.

While you can't ever have a perfect credit score, being mindful of what makes up the score should allow you to work toward establishing a solid one. As shown, the first two items above make up the majority of the score, so at the very least, focus on paying your bills on time and keeping the balances down. Also, don't open a ton of new cards at once. If you do all of that, over time, you'll see your creditworthiness improve and your score slowly creep north.

Key Takeaways:

1. IT'S IMPORTANT TO ESTABLISH CREDIT HISTORY. HAVING NO CREDIT HISTORY CAN HAVE A NEGATIVE EFFECT ON YOUR CREDIT SCORE AND OVERALL CREDITWORTHINESS.

2. BECOME FAMILIAR WITH ALL THE TERMS AND FEES ASSOCIATED WITH CREDIT CARDS. NOT ALL CARDS ARE CREATED EQUALLY, SO MAKE SURE THE CARD THAT YOU HAVE, OR ARE APPLYING FOR, IS RIGHT FOR YOU.

3. IF YOU ARE IN CREDIT CARD DEBT, DIG INTO YOUR SPENDING HABITS FROM THE LAST THREE MONTHS AND USE THAT INFORMATION TO CREATE A PLAN TO PAY DOWN AND EVENTUALLY ELIMINATE YOUR DEBT ENTIRELY. CHECK OUT RESOURCES FROM DAVE RAMSEY OR SUZE ORMAN FOR MORE DETAILED STEPS ON HOW TO DO THIS. IF YOU'RE FEELING UNDERWATER BASED ON YOUR CURRENT DEBT, PLEASE SEEK OUT A CREDIT COUNSELING SERVICE TO HELP YOU WITH A MORE FORMAL PAYOFF PLAN.

4. KNOW YOUR CREDIT SCORE AND WAYS TO INCREASE IT. YOU CREDIT SCORE IS COMPRISED OF THE FOLLOWING: DEBT-TO-CREDIT RATIO, PAYMENT HISTORY, LENGTH OF CREDIT HISTORY, AMOUNT OF NEW CREDIT AND CREDIT MIX.

Chapter Nine

HOW DO I FIND BALANCE IN LIFE?

While in school, the term "wellness" may have referred to the quality of your schedule, the amount of times you went to the gym, and how many times you visited the health center on campus. Perhaps it's already taken on a more robust meaning for you. If it hasn't yet, in the coming years, you'll realize not just how important overall wellness is but that it encompasses much more than just how you look, what the scale says, and what size clothes you wear. It's actually more about the person inside those clothes and how the person on that scale feels on the inside. There are many layers to wellness, but we'll hit on eight major ones: Financial, Physical, Social, Emotional, Spiritual, Mental, Professional and Intellectual. Keep in mind that each person defines "wellness" in a personal way, so feel free to add to the eight areas that we'll focus on in the coming pages.

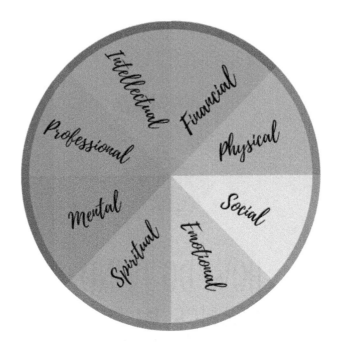

WHERE ARE YOU NOW?

We're going to explore each area of wellness in more detail. After reading each section, rate yourself from 1-10. Think about where you are now within each category. While you're going through this exercise, you may notice that certain areas of wellness seem to be more important to you than others. Each person will assign more or less value to different areas of wellness depending on what's most significant to them. Keep in mind that this wheel won't ever be fully balanced. And that's okay! There should be intentional imbalance in these areas. Maybe you're a former athlete and being in great physical health is a non-negotiable for you. Maybe right now you're an 8 in physical health and you decide to get that number to a 10. You may choose to forgo focus in one area to double down efforts on the physical wellness space. Perhaps you miss some social activities to train for that marathon or take out savings to hire a personal trainer. Someone who cares about physical health to a lesser degree may be at a 5, and a 7 rating may be all they ever strive for. This rating is personal, and it's about living in alignment to what wellness means for you.

Knowing that everyone's personal definition of wellness will differ, avoid the temptation to begin comparing yourself to others. You may look at someone else and size them up in one of these areas without knowing the full story. For example, someone you work with may appear to be very wealthy while you're barely making ends meet. This is especially true if they're more established in their career. You cannot compare your "Chapter 1" with someone else's "Chapter 10;" it's not unreasonable for someone deeper into his or her career to be more financially stable than you. Having said that, you have no idea what's really going on behind closed doors. They may rate themselves a 2 in the area of financial wellness because they're in deep debt trying to maintain what appears to be a glamorous lifestyle. Plus, they may be working long hours and looking longingly at your social life, trying to remember the last time they got together with good friends. Similarly, you may be struggling with your weight and see someone who is in peak physical shape. Hard to not to compare, right? Any idea how her spiritual or social wellness is doing? Of course not; we have no idea what others are going through. Before you spend energy comparing yourself to others, keep in mind that everyone has their own definition of what "balanced" looks like and it's up to us to keep realigning each facet of wellness when we feel one is out of whack.

Now let's explore each wellness aspect in more detail.

SPIRITUAL

Find meaning in life events, demonstrate individual purpose, and live a life that reflects your values and beliefs.

Often a life change causes a person to pause a bit and try to understand the meaning behind the change. Maybe you've lost a job or a loved one has passed away. Maybe you go through a bad breakup with the person you were sure was going to be the "one." You may start to wonder why these things happened and, as part of your healing process, seek an explanation from an event that may have left you emotionally scarred. Your quest for purpose can be a lifelong journey, one that you may never finish. But those who find comfort during the journey seem to benefit from this quest, even if the answer isn't as clear as they'd hoped. You can turn to religion, personal development, and other areas to start to explore ideas that appear bigger than yourself. If you can connect who you are to something bigger than yourself and, in turn, live a life that reflects your values and beliefs, you'll feel a sense of fulfillment that you'll be happy you have.

EMOTIONAL

Have a positive attitude, a high self-esteem, a strong sense of self, and the ability to recognize and share a wide range of feelings with others in a constructive way.

Getting to know yourself is a critical component of wellness. Understanding who you are, what you value and appreciate, and why you are the way you are vital components to true emotional wellness. When someone asks how you are and your automatic response is "fine," think about whether there's a more fitting word to use. Are you just "fine," or is there a better way to describe how you're feeling, not for their benefit but for your own?

Having control of your emotional vocabulary and saying you're "frustrated" when you're frustrated and "overwhelmed" when you're overwhelmed or "fantastic" when you're fantastic will add to your overall wellness. Allowing yourself to feel a wide range of feelings and share those feelings with others is healthy, particularly when it's shared in a constructive way. You should also be mindful of the words you use when talking to yourself. What are the first things that come out of your mouth when you look in the mirror each morning? Do you beat yourself up over every mistake you make, calling yourself dumb for having messed up, or do you give yourself a little grace and learn from the error? We would never talk to people we love in a demeaning tone; why is it acceptable to talk to ourselves like that? Be kind to yourself, because if you aren't, it's going to be hard for you to fully accept kindness from those around you.

MENTAL

Realize your own abilities, cope with the normal stresses of life, work productively and fruitfully, and make a contribution to your community.

Many graduates have never had to deal with all of the new stresses and pressures that come with "adulting" before. Sure, there was stress in college, and while I'm not minimizing past stress or anxiety that you've experienced, the new challenges you face in this area may be more difficult for you to manage. If you're feeling weighed down by the pressures of your post-college life, please talk about it. Share how you're feeling with friends and family.

Recognizing the feelings you have and speaking them out loud to others is a great first step toward getting a handle on your mental wellness. Sometimes even a simple five-minute break from what you're doing can improve your well-being. Removing yourself from the stressful situation to take a breath may be all you need to come back to the circumstances with a clearer mind. Getting outside for a walk, taking a lunch break by yourself, or heading out of town for a long weekend can help you reset a bit and come back feeling more refreshed than before you left. Spend time doing something you love that doesn't generate the feelings of overwhelm and stress that you may be feeling. Calling a friend or re-engaging with the hobby that you've left on pause will do wonders for your mental wellness.

If these tips aren't helping, it may be time to speak with a licensed professional. The vast network of therapy is there to help you, and finding a therapist that specializes in your demographic, gender, or specific situation can be one of the best moves you've ever made. If you have insurance, start there. Call the member services hotline on the back of your card or log onto their website to learn more about the type of coverage you have with your current plan. There are many therapists who take insurance and many others who don't. In the event you don't find a match with one of the therapists in your insurance network, you may need to expand your search. If you are in the United States, head over to physchologytoday.com to conduct a search of therapists in your area. This site is also packed with helpful articles and resources that may aid in your healing as well.

Asking for referrals is another option to explore. Check with your primary care physician and ask them if they'd refer a colleague of theirs. Unfortunately there is still a stigma attached to therapy, so it's not talked about as often as it should be, but if you're comfortable enough asking trusted friends and family for referrals, do it! More people go to therapy than you think. Just as you'd ask for their recommendation for a dentist or optometrist they love, you can do the same with a therapist. And just as with your physical health, mental health is an area that cannot be ignored.

PROFESSIONAL

Seek to have a career that is interesting, enjoyable, meaningful, and which contributes to the larger society.

So you got hired at the company of your dreams, but maybe you're not in the position of your dreams, at least not yet. Right now, you are probably only qualified for an entry-level position, nothing more. And that's okay; as a recent grad, you are entry-level! But after a little while you'll want to grow at that company or another in the industry of your choice.

If I were to ask you right now about the two biggest threats facing your industry, what would you say? Who are your company's biggest competitors, and what are the value differentiators between your company and theirs? Who are the most influential people in your industry? Do you follow them on social media? What articles have they been featured in, and have you read them? It's okay if you don't know these answers right now. But start your research. Today. Knowing this information will be paramount in your ability to grow and advance. And taking the initiative to discover this information will look favorable for you.

Stay well-versed in your craft. Think about it like a sport: if you played basketball in high school, you didn't just walk onto the varsity team without ever having picked up a ball. Chances are, your parents signed you up when you were four or five years old. Those early classes were focused on fundamentals. You learned to dribble and play defense, and at some point, you figured out how to shoot the ball at least in the vicinity of the basket. But as you know, there's much more to the game than just dribbling. So you evolved and learned more advanced skills. Your practices got more demanding, and you started acquiring new skills that, as an entry-level player, you couldn't imagine doing.

Same goes with your career; you should always be learning and growing. While you're interviewing, ask your potential employer about options for continuing education and training. Some companies will pay for you to attend courses that are relevant for your career. If you're a software developer, I'm not sure that your boss will sponsor you to attend a photography class, but I bet she would be open to you going to an event sponsored by technology leaders, especially if you'll come back knowing more that you can, in turn, apply to your daily work. That investment made by your employer should come back to your company in the long run. Conversely, how do you think your boss would feel if you paid to attend your own training? Or if you found a watered-down version of a national training locally or virtually? It shows your initiative and a desire to learn and better yourself, something that should impress every boss. Also, if you ever get to a point where you feel the need to explore other job options, you now have connections with others in a similar industry. And, how nice would it be to take your resume to an event where the "Who's Who" in your industry hangs out versus submitting to a black-hole email address like jobs@ thecompanyofyourdreams.com?

I have been able to do several educational courses over the years by volunteering for different opportunities at my company. There are usually one to two company-sponsored management courses you can take each year. I always made sure to talk with my managers about my desire to participate in any sort of self-improvement or management course. I think those opportunities are valuable because you get to network and show your leadership team your desire to learn."

- Eric, University of California San Diego, Class of 2006

If your company won't pay for you to attend a fancy event that costs a lot of money and requires time off of work, find one that meets on your own time. Have you heard of Meetup.com? That's a great way to connect with people who are interested in what you're into. Whether it's for personal or professional reasons, these events are often free to attend. It's also a great way to meet other people with common interests in your area. Additionally, you can check out a local community college or search online for "free (insert specialty here) class," and you'll come up with a ton. Often, training companies offer free content. Their hope is that you will like what you see, build some trust with the company, and then eventually pay for a higher-level class or course. And maybe over time you will decide to invest in a course, but for now, be grateful for the wealth of free info out there.

Put yourself out there. Take the initiative and keep learning. You'll be happy that you did.

SHOULD YOU GO TO GRAD SCHOOL?

The decision of whether or not to supplement your formal education and earn a degree beyond the one you earned in undergrad is a very personal choice in some cases; in others, the field of study you're pursuing may require it. For those who don't "need" it but may want it, you've got to assess whether or not you want to explore this option right now, at some point in the future, or at all. It's worth doing some research and seeing the professional benefits of the degree. If you don't need it, what will obtaining the degree do for you? Will you make more money, get promotions faster, etc.? Do your best to find examples of those who are in a similar field and are a few years ahead of you. Family, friends, and past graduates could shed some light in this area. Ask yourself: will this degree open up new job opportunities for me? Will it open up job opportunities with higher pay?

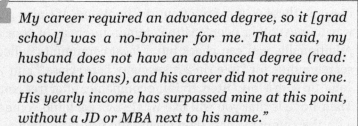

My career required an advanced degree, so it [grad school] was a no-brainer for me. That said, my husband does not have an advanced degree (read: no student loans), and his career did not require one. His yearly income has surpassed mine at this point, without a JD or MBA next to his name."

- Sarah, Boston University, Class of 2005

I have my master's because I have no choice in my field (in order to be an occupational therapist, you need a master's degree in this field). I learned everything I know and use every day during my time at NYU and made awesome, driven, motivated friends along the way. However, I will say it is EXPENSIVE. I would recommend thinking long and hard before going for an advanced degree due to the high cost."

- Erika, Pennsylvania State University, Class of 2014

Even if you don't need an advanced degree for your profession, you may want to pursue a graduate degree for personal reasons. Maybe you have a desire to gain a higher-level understanding of a totally unrelated subject. Go for it! Check out both in-person and online options to see if the class schedules and costs make sense for you.

Four more years of schooling isn't cheap, no matter where you go. Perhaps getting a few years of work under your belt and then making the decision whether to go back to school is the right move for you. Many companies offer some sort of tuition reimbursement program, especially if the advanced degree you're pursuing is in line with the role you hold at the company. If you're going to explore this, be sure to check on the terms of the program. If the company contributes to your tuition and then you leave the company within a certain window, often you're required to pay some or all of that reimbursement back.

> *I decided to get my MBA a few years after I graduated undergrad. I wanted to make sure it was actually what I wanted, and I also wanted some valuable work under my belt first. It helped frame my future role as Executive Director of a nonprofit in a way that proved to be super impactful! However, I paid for it myself and worked my full-time job through it, taking professional MBA classes at night. Looking back, I learned more from the process than the content but wouldn't change it."*
>
> - Maria, University of Missouri, Class of 2010

INTELLECTUAL

Be open to new ideas, be creative, think critically, and seek out new challenges.

You may decide that more formal schooling and advanced degrees aren't for you. Perhaps there's no professional benefit and, personally, you have no interest in an advanced degree. If that's you, that's totally fine. Just know that even though school is over, it's still in your best interest to continue to learn. You will be put in situations—both inside and outside of work—where you're in a different type of "classroom." In this setting, there's no master syllabus or textbooks, but there are professors and tests. These professors show up in the forms of bosses, mentors, or friends, and the tests you experience will be harder than the ones you had in school. And without being overly dramatic, it's not a matter of "if" you get tested, it's a matter of "when." You'll have to learn to cope with love and loss, highs and lows, success and defeat. Your mental fitness here will be critical.

If you're open to non-accredited instruction on a specific subject matter, you've got endless possibilities. If you're interested in a deeper knowledge of art and art history, for example, you could spend your weekends at museums and take trips that will expose you to different artists and forms of art. You could look into a part-time paid or volunteer job at an art-related establishment. If you want to create art, you could sign up for drawing, painting, or sculpting classes. You could apply this approach to other skills you'd like to learn, such as dance, photography, writing, film-making, a foreign language, etc. There are virtual options for learning all around us. A Google search will reveal many avenues you can choose to advance your knowledge in a particular area.

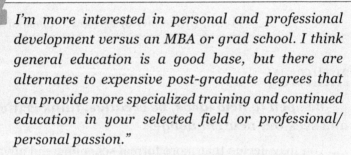

I'm more interested in personal and professional development versus an MBA or grad school. I think general education is a good base, but there are alternates to expensive post-graduate degrees that can provide more specialized training and continued education in your selected field or professional/ personal passion."

- Nikki, James Madison University, Class of 2005

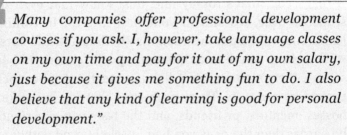

Many companies offer professional development courses if you ask. I, however, take language classes on my own time and pay for it out of my own salary, just because it gives me something fun to do. I also believe that any kind of learning is good for personal development."

- Steven, University of Connecticut, Class of 2016

> " In my opinion, personal and professional development should be life goals for everyone. It doesn't mean you have to constantly get a raise or a promotion or move to a new company. Regardless of the company you're a part of, the title you hold or the season of life you are in, you should be aspiring to learn and grow. When we are stagnant with our passion and learning, the rest of our life grows stale and loses meaning."
>
> - Daniel, University of Maryland, 2008

One way to expand your knowledge is to find some people you admire both at work and in your personal life and ask them what they're reading. And when I say "reading," I mean consuming information in whatever way you can. While I love curling up with a good book, how often does that really happen? I have a chair in my master bedroom that is super cozy and comfy and perfect for "curling up with a good book." But do you know how many times I've sat there and read a book? Exactly zero times. None.

Most of my "reading" and learning happen via my ear, with the help of audiobooks and podcasts. Many people say they don't read because they don't have time. This is why audio learning is so great. I take existing activities and add learning on top. Most of the time spent in my car is listening to books that are going to make me a better version of myself in all areas of my life: as a wife, as a mom, as a coach, as a leader, as a friend, and as a person. When I'm folding laundry or drying my hair in the morning, I'm filling my head with great info. And even if you don't want to listen to books while doing the activities I mentioned above, think about how much mindless scrolling happens on a daily basis. Reallocating even ten minutes of your screen time toward knocking out a few pages of a great book will be time well spent. It is a far better use of your time than looking through an Instagram feed at some influencer's highlight reel.

Instead of looking at them and wanting to be them, read a book and take some action on becoming a better you!

> **Soak up all the professional development you can, even if it's TED Talks or podcasts, especially if you're still looking for jobs. They want to see that you're willing to learn and can apply what you've already learned."**
>
> — Brittany, Millersville University, Class of 2012

Book recommendations can be found on pages 197-209 if you're interested in exploring some new options

FINANCIAL

Find satisfaction with current and future financial situations.

Chapters six, seven, and eight dive deeper into this area, but financial wellness is critical for overall happiness. That does not mean that you have to be wealthy to be happy. It does mean that you need to make enough money to support your basic needs and ideally have enough left for some of your "wants" as well. The goal is to live within your means and learn to manage your finances for the short and long term.

Dave Ramsey, previously referenced in chapter five, writes a lot about the idea of "financial stress." The American Physiological Association found that 72 percent of Americans feel stressed about money at least some of the time, and almost 25 percent categorize themselves as "extremely stressed." Almost 80 percent of Americans are living paycheck to paycheck, and, in addition to seeing their bank account balances decline day after day, they also experience feelings of anxiety, worry, guilt, denial, insomnia, and panic attacks that can arise from financial stress. If you bring bad financial habits into a relationship with a significant other, it is possible that money will become a point of frustration later in the relationship. Many couples cite "finances" as the number one topic they argue about.

Ramsey suggests four steps to get out of financial stress:

1. **Take inventory.** Face your bills head-on. It will be scary, but it needs to be done. Get a good idea of where you really stand.

2. **Make and stick to a budget.** More information on creating a budget can be found in chapter six.

3. **Pay off all debt** and start establishing your emergency fund and long-term savings.

4. **Practice gratitude.** Be grateful for what you have and stop comparing what you have (or don't have) to what someone else has. Not only is comparison a joy-killer, trying to "keep up with the Joneses" can also cause you to fall further into debt, creating even more stress.

Money doesn't create happiness. That's for sure. But the mismanagement of money can certainly take away from that happiness.

SOCIAL

Build personal relationships with others, deal with conflict appropriately, and connect to a positive social network.

Whether built in person or through a virtual channel like FaceTime or social media, the need for social interaction is critical for our overall wellness. Being surrounded by a positive social network will automatically have a positive effect on your life. The same can be said for the opposite. Many self-help experts have taken their own spin on the idea that you become a product of the five people you spend the most time with. Look around you. Who are you surrounding yourself with? Are they mostly positive or negative? When you spend time with them, do you leave feeling uplifted and happy or are you emotionally drained? If you are already thinking of a few people in your immediate circle that are zapping some of your energy, rest assured you don't need to completely cut these people out of your life. However, it is important that you recognize how you feel when you're with a certain group of people and manage your time with them accordingly. No matter how busy you are, always look for ways to make time for those you care most about. Continually investing in your relationships and your social connections will add to your life in more ways than you can imagine.

PHYSICAL

Take care of your body for optimal health and functioning.

In college, my primary motivator for working out and trying to eat well was purely surface level. I wanted to look good in my outfits for the weekend, be able to rock a bikini for spring break, and just feel healthy overall. And while I still want to rock bikinis and feel good, health takes on a whole different meaning now. As you age (and see your parents age), you often realize just how critical taking care of your physical and mental health is.

I feel like after college is when I really started to pay attention to my health, both mental and physical. I've become incredibly passionate about a natural lifestyle."

- Lindsay, Temple University, Class of 2006

GET OUT THERE AND MOVE

Many of you reading this book were probably fortunate enough to enjoy the perks of a free membership to your university gym or recreation center. These facilities often offer racks and racks of free weights, a variety of cardio equipment, and plenty of group fitness classes to choose from. The classes were likely offered around the clock, and, based on your schedule of only having class for a few hours each day, taking one of these classes may have been easier than it is now. After all, they were free, and you had the free time to take advantage of them. However, if you begin working full-time during "normal business hours," getting to the gym can sometimes prove to be difficult.

> " *I gained a shit-ton of weight after college because I wasn't walking anymore and was also not eating well. My health was fine, but I was chubby and in need of vegetables for sure. I started running, doing workout videos in the office with my co-workers, and taking yoga classes. All that got me back in shape in my mid-20s."*
>
> – Tricia, Boston University, Class of 1998

> " *I was smart about making sure I planned workouts during my stressful days of teaching. I took the classes with friends as both a health and social outlet. We joined the YMCA, which actually has kickass classes and offers discounts to teachers!"*
>
> - Maria, University of Missouri, Class of 2010

Whether you can find the pockets of time to go to a gym or you decide to work out from home, moving your body daily is critical. Many times it's the last thing you want to do. After all, you've been working all day and may not "feel" like working out. Even if you don't feel like it, sneak in thirty minutes of movement each day. Why move daily? Because regular exercise is beneficial in so many ways! In addition to physical results that come in the form of weight loss and clothes fitting better, there are many other benefits that come from prioritizing your fitness. Here are some of the more common benefits of a consistent workout routine:

BENEFITS OF DAILY EXERCISE

1. Lowers risk of various ailments, including high blood pressure, diabetes, common colds, and other long-term conditions.

2. Keeps your brain and body fit and boosts your mental health.

3. Opportunity to work with multiple clients at once 3. Lifts your mood and reduces stress.

4. Improves sleep patterns and lessens fatigue while awake.

5. Reduces feelings of depression and helps to alleviate anxiety.

6. Improves joint functions and muscle strength and strengthens your bones and heart.

7. Improves eating habits and overall appetite.

8. Improves balance, flexibility, and coordination while boosting your immune system.

9. Increases your endurance and energy and provides an increased oxygen supply to your cells.

10. Increases sex drive and satisfaction—yes, please!

YOUR DAILY CHOICES ADD UP

We've talked about the Compound Effect as it relates to money, but it can be applied to your health as well. Let's talk about someone who makes poor food choices versus someone who is making smart choices. Making poor choices one day may not be such a big deal that day, or the day after, or even the week after that. But doing this consistently over time may add up to health problems that cost you more than you ever expected to pay in the form of medical bills, higher health insurance premiums, and medications that are required just to keep your body operating at a "normal" level.

And here's the thing: you don't lose weight overnight. You don't gain it overnight, either. You slowly put on weight over time, one bad decision after another, and the next thing you know, you're heavier and unhealthier than you've ever been. Pay attention to your small habits. This awareness will help you catch potential problems before they arise. You can attack the dollar menu at a fast-food joint and for $5 walk out with a couple of burgers, fries, a million-ounce soda, and a shake. You leave full, and you only spent $5. You have to pay two to three times that amount for a healthy salad at Panera. And you don't even get fries and a shake with that. But this isn't just about today. It's about all of the food choices you make this week and this month and this year. They're either helping your body or hurting it.

I gained weight right after college. I never got the 'Freshman 15' in school; I gained weight once I started working full-time. The hours killed me, so I never went to the gym and never felt like cooking a healthy meal."

- Portia, Florida Atlantic University, Class of 2002

It took me about a year post-college to get my health on track. I was a collegiate athlete, and when the sport ended for me, I lost my will to work out and my identity all at once. Got to my heaviest weight around 289 pounds, which was hard being that I used to be this all-American athlete who could now barely walk up the stairs! Thankfully, however, I was able to find a program, a community, and support that worked for me. I changed up my nutrition, took up kickboxing and then CrossFit, and eventually found the world of Women's Professional Football. It's been an amazing journey since then."

- Brilynn, NYIT, Class of 2009

I had a tough time fitting in workouts with my very busy job and social schedule. I generally worked out early in the mornings; I would get to the gym when it opened at 5:30 a.m. and then shower there and go straight to the office. Food was much more challenging; I lived on take-out and meals out. Along with the drinking that came along with going out with friends frequently, this caused me to gain weight during my first year of practice."

- Sarah, Boston University, Class of 2005

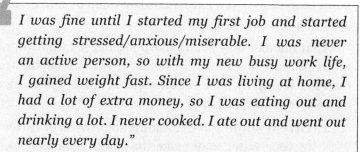

> *I was fine until I started my first job and started getting stressed/anxious/miserable. I was never an active person, so with my new busy work life, I gained weight fast. Since I was living at home, I had a lot of extra money, so I was eating out and drinking a lot. I never cooked. I ate out and went out nearly every day."*
>
> – Mike, Ohio State University, Class of 2015

> *I gained weight when I got my first job. I wasn't used to the long days and wasn't a good cook, so I gained weight after college thanks to lots of happy hours, going out every weekend night, and eating horribly because I didn't want to cook. I had a gym membership... I went twice during that year. I was a train wreck."*
>
> – Ashley, James Madison University, Class of 2005

LET'S TALK ABOUT YOUR DRINKING PROBLEM

Can we quickly address a drinking problem that many new graduates (and adults for that matter) have? No, no, not the same one you may have had in college when splitting a case of Natty Light with your buddy seemed like a sound decision. I'm talking about a magical liquid that helps fuel your muscles, rids your body of toxins, gives your brain a boost, and greases your joints, all while helping with clearer skin and calorie control. I'm talking about WATER, my friends. And you should be drinking it. A lot of it. All throughout the day. The rule of thumb is that you should be drinking half of your body weight, in ounces, each day. And if you're a coffee drinker, you should replace each ounce of coffee that you drink with an equivalent amount of water. You're 150 pounds? Aim to drink 75 ounces of water daily, and if you have a 20-ounce cup of coffee each day, bring that goal up to 95 ounces.

That number may sound like a lot, but it's what your body needs to function at optimal levels. If you are having trouble reaching that daily goal, follow some of these tips to increase your water intake each day:

1. **Give it some flavor.** Adding some fresh or frozen fruit to your water may make the "boring" taste of water a little more fun.

2. **Get a water bottle that you like and that helps you with your daily goal.** There are some fun ones out there. Some have measurements on the outside, letting you know each time you've downed another ten ounces. The Hydro Flask lights up every once in a while to remind you to get a few sips in. A reusable water bottle is not only better for the environment, but if you have it with you constantly, you're more likely to drink. If it's out of sight, it's likely that it will quickly be out of mind.

3. **Use an app to track your daily cups.** There are many free apps out there that allow you to track your daily intake. These apps often come with reminders and alerts that you can set so you get pinged throughout the day to remind you to take a swig. There is something rewarding about seeing the progress. Whether you're checking boxes or crossing off pictures of water bottles, seeing your progress throughout the day can add some extra motivation to your goal.

4. **Drink before each meal.** Downing eight to ten ounces of water about a half-hour before each meal can help you chip away at your daily goal. Additionally, you don't go into each meal starving. Often, we confuse thirst for hunger. This is also a good thing to keep in mind throughout the day. If you're feeling hungry, first think about the last time you drank a glass of water. If it's been a while, down a glass and see if the "hunger" goes away.

5. **Practice one-for-one drinking when going out.** On nights that you're going out to enjoy some adult beverages, make sure you're grabbing a glass of water in between alcoholic drinks. Not only will this help keep you hydrated, you're more likely to save some money on your bar tab and have less of a hangover the next day.

6. **Keep full water bottles handy.** The presence of a full water bottle may be all you need to keep your mind focused on getting in enough water. I always have a water bottle with me and some extras in my car, at my desk, and in my bags. As soon as one is empty, I fill it up. For me, this increases the likelihood I'll drain the cup.

7. **Get some fun reusable straws.** Many people say that using a straw helps them drink more. There are some great ones out there, easy to clean and take on the go. Many water bottles now include straws that are attached to the water bottle itself to help aid in this process.

8. **Tie your water goal to other actions you currently do.** In his book *Atomic Habits*, James Clear talks about the concept of "habit stacking," which suggests that we should tie new habits we're trying to form to existing habits that are already part of our daily routine. If you get up and immediately brush your teeth, for instance, have a glass of water waiting next to your toothbrush. Now you'll drink a glass of water after you complete your existing habit of brushing your teeth.

9. **Get a group of friends involved in your goal.** Talk to your friends and get them in on a water challenge. Start a text thread or WhatsApp group chat, and make it a little competition. Take pictures of your empty water bottles or send GIFs back and forth when you hit your goals.

10. **Reward yourself for hitting your goal.** Put some sort of reward in place when you meet your daily goal or when you hit your goals seven days in a row. Maybe you throw $5 in a jar, watch it grow week over week, and then take that money and celebrate with a larger purchase or a round of "not water" drinking with your friends.

SLEEP YOUR WAY TO GREAT HEALTH

Now that many of you have gone from a schedule which requires you to be in class a few hours a day to one that requires you to be in an office for eight to ten hours per day, getting a great night's sleep is even more crucial. The American Academy of Sleep Medicine states that one in three Americans don't get enough sleep. A night or two of this isn't the end of the world. However, a pattern of interrupted sleep or too few hours a night can add up to longer-term problems, while adequate sleep has a host of benefits.

Wouldn't it be cool if you could lose weight in your sleep? Well, it's possible! Great sleep is crucial when it comes to reaching and eventually maintaining a healthy weight. Too little sleep triggers a spike in cortisol, which is a stress hormone that tells your body to conserve energy to fuel you at a later time. A University of Chicago study states that four days of missed sleep can lead to a drop in the amount of insulin that your body produces. Insulin is a hormone that is needed to change sugar, starches, and other food into energy. And if your body doesn't have enough insulin, it stores these foods as fat, and you'll hang onto the excess weight that you're trying to lose. In addition to being harder to lose weight, here are some other problems that can result from a sleep deficit:

1. **You're more likely to get sick:** There is a direct relationship between sleep and your immune system. If your immune system is compromised, you're more likely to get sick. When you've had a string of nights in a row where sleep isn't great, you'll be more susceptible to getting sick. The lack of sleep can impact your body's ability to fight off illness, so you may get sicker easier than someone who's had more consistent rest. Additionally, if you do get sick, it can be harder to fight off.

2. **You make unhealthy choices:** When you're tired, your body craves caffeine, sugar, and carbohydrates for quick bursts of energy, so you'll generally reach for these food items over more sensible choices like lean proteins

and vegetables. The lack of sleep also makes it harder to stick to previously-set plans, such as healthy meals, scheduled workouts, etc. Suddenly, you're too tired to cook and may opt for something easier, more convenient, and often less healthy. The gym class that you planned on attending after work doesn't seem possible because you're just so tired. Decisions like these, over time, can add up to weight gain.

3. **Your thinking and cognition is negatively affected:** Repeated poor sleep can lead to major cognition issues. Your reaction time and alertness is compromised, your decision-making is off, and your reasoning and problem-solving skills aren't as sharp as they should be. Additionally, learning and committing things to memory become harder. Proper rest enables your brain to lock in any new information it learned that day and commit it to long-term memory. Those all-nighters before a big exam may work in the short term, but that's certainly not a sound long-term strategy for learning.

4. **You become more accident-prone:** The National Sleep Foundation has found that you're three times more likely to be involved in an automobile accident if you get six hours of sleep or less per night. This risk increases if you work a lot of overtime, perform shift work, and drive as a main requirement of your job.

Moral of the story? Make sleep a priority. I know it can be hard with all the binge-watching opportunities out there, but there's a time and a place for that. Planning out your day, including your wake and sleep time, will help you find a way to fit it all in. If you plan it well, you should be able to get to and from work, enjoy time with friends or family post-work, and still get to bed at a reasonable time. If you're finding it difficult to shut it down at a reasonable time, here are a few suggestions that may help you start dreaming a little earlier:

1. **Shut down technology at least one hour before bed.** Even after we put down the phone or turn off the TV, our minds are still going. Fully "shutting down" becomes more difficult when we're thinking about the ending of the show or an email you just received from your boss. Separating sleep from technology can be a challenge, especially when many of us have TVs and smartphones in our bedrooms. When possible, use an alarm clock instead of your phone, and charge your phone in a different room or in your room but out of reach from your bed. This will help prevent you from mindlessly reaching for it out of habit instead of necessity. Your bedroom should be used for sleeping and sex—that's it. Keeping it reserved for those two purposes will help your mind and body get into the habit of getting right to bed when you enter the room.

2. **Create a bedtime ritual.** A repeatable pattern that you put into motion each night will help you create good habits around getting to sleep. Reading or meditating are better options than knocking out a bit more work before you turn in for the night. Often, we're not as alert as we should be by that point, so any work we finish may not be done with the high quality we'd like. Plus, as mentioned above, once you shut the laptop off or put your pen down, your mind is still working, and the chances of you quickly falling asleep are low. It's better to call it a night and set your alarm for a tad earlier to finish the tasks when you're more alert and ready to begin your day.

3. **Watch your food/caffeine intake throughout the day.** Eating fried foods or foods that are harder to digest can cause discomfort at night, especially if you turn in right after dinner. Eating a large meal and then immediately lying down can lead to indigestion, heartburn, and other forms of discomfort. Caffeine can also linger in your system for five to six hours, so that afternoon cup of coffee that you grabbed before leaving the office or the soda that you had with dinner could

prevent you from falling asleep at a reasonable time. If you tend to have caffeinated drinks later in the day, it may be wise to experiment with not consuming any after a certain point in the day or removing them from your diet completely.

4. **Ensure your environment is dark and conducive to sleep.** The glow of the television or other lights in the room can prevent you from falling into a deep sleep. When you're in a dark environment, your body releases melatonin, a natural hormone that regulates the sleep/wake cycle. Everyone has a different level of sensitivity to lights when it comes to their bedrooms, so experiment to find what level of darkness you need to sleep soundly. If you find that you need a totally pitch-black environment, investing in blackout shades and covering any lights omitting from electronics in your room can help. Shutting everything down, including the lights, will signal your body that it's time to get some shuteye.

WHAT DOES "WORK/LIFE BALANCE" MEAN, ANYWAY?

"Work/life balance" is a term that may be newer for you now that you've got a full-time job that's requiring your attention during most of your waking hours. Throwing all of yourself into your job while sacrificing other areas of your wellness may work for a little while, but eventually it will catch up with you. You'll feel burnt out and may make negative career decisions based on this feeling. Quitting your job may not be the solution. You may be able to make small changes in your schedule to work in the areas of wellness that feel like they're lacking. If you're working crazy late hours, getting out to a happy hour or taking a long weekend with friends may help re-energize you and fill your "social" bucket just enough to keep you going.

WHAT IF YOU GET A FLAT TIRE?

Pretend you are driving a car and it has eight tires, one tire dedicated to each area of wellness. What if one or two started to go flat a bit? How would that affect the performance of the car? At first, you may not notice, but if you don't stop to re-inflate the tires that have lost some air, eventually the car will become impossible to drive. You'll literally and figuratively crash. The same is true if one tire is overinflated. Eventually, that tire will burst, and the entire car will be negatively impacted. Make sure all of the wellness areas are balanced and if necessary, pull over and assess each "tire." If needed, add some "air" where needed and realign those tires, continuing to drive forward. Suddenly with the right focus and attention, you'll find yourself behind the wheel of a high-performance vehicle.

Key takeaways:

1. WELLNESS IS FAR MORE THAN JUST HOW PHYSICALLY FIT YOU ARE. IT HAS MANY LAYERS IN ADDITION TO YOUR PHYSICAL WELLNESS, INCLUDING INTELLECTUAL, PROFESSIONAL, MENTAL, SPIRITUAL, SOCIAL, EMOTIONAL, AND FINANCIAL WELLNESS.

2. DO A GUT CHECK AND ASSESS WHERE YOU ARE NOW IN EACH OF THESE AREAS, AND THEN DETERMINE WHICH AREAS YOU WANT TO IMPROVE. NOT ALL AREAS NEED TO BE A "10," BUT IT'S IMPORTANT TO FEEL LIKE YOU'VE GOT A HANDLE IN ALL OF THESE AREAS.

3. IF YOU'RE HAVING DIFFICULTY IMPROVING YOUR MENTAL WELLNESS, MAKE SURE YOU INVOLVE OTHERS IN YOUR HEALING PROCESS. TALK TO FRIENDS, FAMILY, AND MENTAL HEALTH PROFESSIONALS WHO ARE ABLE TO ASSIST YOU IN THE STEPS NEEDED TO WORK TOWARD A HEALTHIER MENTAL WELL-BEING.

4. YOUR DAILY CHOICES ADD UP. PAY ATTENTION TO HOW OFTEN YOU'RE MOVING YOUR BODY, IF YOU'RE FUELING AND HYDRATING IT CORRECTLY, AND THE QUALITY OF YOUR SLEEP. ALL OF THESE WORK TOGETHER TO HELP YOU REACH A STATE OF OPTIMAL PHYSICAL WELLNESS THAT ALSO POSITIVELY IMPACTS OTHER AREAS OF WELLNESS.

5. WHEN FEELING UNBALANCED, TAKE A STEP BACK, BREATHE, AND ASSESS WHERE YOU GOT "OUT OF WHACK." SOMETIMES ALL YOU NEED IS A FEW CHANGES TO FEEL MORE BALANCED AGAIN.

6. CONTINUE TO WORK TOWARD AN OPTIMAL BALANCE FOR YOU, NOT OTHERS IN YOUR LIFE.

PARTING THOUGHTS

Okay, are you ready now to enter adulthood? Or at least a little more "ready" than you were before you cracked open this book? If you are reading this, congratulations! You made it to the end. Your mind may be overwhelmed with all the "do this" and "don't do that" and "be sure to never do this" suggestions. After taking in all of this information, know that you're going to get some things wrong. And that's okay. That is, as they say, "life."

And part of the beauty of life is found in the mess. The real lessons we learn in life cannot be found in a book like this. They're in the experiences—the good ones and the bad. It's making the wrong career move and learning how to course correct and position yourself better for your next job. It's allowing your spending to get a little out of control and learning how to reel it back in and get yourself in a better financial spot. It's buying a car that's probably a bit out of your price range, but enjoying the hell out of it before you get a bit wiser and trade it in for something a bit more practical.

Your early 20s are an interesting time. Even though you technically were an adult at 18, you're really "adulting" for the first time. You've got a newfound set of responsibilities, which come with some pressures, but you're also making things happen. You're creating a life for yourself. You're building your finances and your career. You're learning how to juggle a schedule that's never required more from you. You are managing more money than ever before, going back and forth between ensuring you can pay for rent and food and fun while trying to be mindful of savings and retirement. It's a lot. More than you've ever balanced before.

So be kind to yourself. Give yourself some grace. Know that plenty of people entered "the real world" before you and, even though they may have done things differently, they made it. Possibly with some bruises and scars, but they made it. They have lived to tell stories about their early 20s, and I'd be willing to bet most of them look back on that time with fond memories. And almost all of them (myself included!) would probably wish we hadn't worried as much as we did.

Although some of you reading this may be parents, the majority of you, I'd imagine, are responsible for just you. And speaking as a 38-year-old mom of three, I can tell you that there's something special about just worrying about you. You are in charge of your time and how you spend it. Your career and how you grow it. Your money and how you manage it. And your life and how you create it.

Before you know it, you'll find yourself approaching new life stages. You'll look back on these years and think, "Man, that was a blast." The hard times won't seem so hard, and the aftermath of the mistakes you made will likely have subsided.

There truly is no other time like this. If you play it right, you'll start to have some padding in your bank account. Save some and spend some. Be selfish. Go out on that date. Take that class. Visit that country. Try that restaurant. Enjoy the hell out of life, would ya?

You've got this.

Alicia

ACKNOWLEDGEMENTS

This book began as just an idea that resulted from a casual conversation with my Dad just over 15 years ago. I've had it on my to-do list since then, working on it here and there when I felt somewhat inspired. And it would have stayed on that list of things to do, that list of dreams that I was going to get to "someday," had it not been for the team around me. Without this crew of cheerleaders, advisors, coaches, mentors and publishing professionals, this book wouldn't be in your hands today.

Honorée Corder, my coach - thank you for publishing *You Must Write A Book* and helping me believe that I must, in fact, write my book. And not only did you help me believe it was possible...you showed me the steps I needed to take in order to make it happen. The lessons you've taught me, about writing and life in general, won't be forgotten. If you have a book on your heart, reach out to Honorée - she will help you turn it into a reality. Thank you for also connecting me with a great team of professionals including editors, Alyssa Archer and Tammi Metzler, proofreader Jackie Dana, designer Dino Marino and copywriter Brian Meeks. The guidance of these experts was invaluable and draft after draft, I'm proud of the finished product and have these individuals to thank.

Thanks to all the past "new graduates" that shared their personal experiences with me, particularly the ones who are quoted in this book: Allison, Allyson, Alyse, Ashley C, Ashley L, Brilynn, Brian, Brittany, Colleen, Daniel, Dave, Diane, Elyse, Eric, Erika, Jacki, Julie, Justin, Kara, Kelly, Kendra, Kyle, Lauren, Lindsay, Maria, Matt, Mary-Paige, Melissa, Mike, Natalie, Nikki, Portia, Preston, Sarah B, Sarah C, Shalon, Stacy, Steven, Taylor, Tracy, and Tricia. Special thanks to Lance Pieper and Chris Bennett for adding professional input and added value for the readers.

Speaking of readers - thank YOU for spending some time with me over the course of this book. There is no commodity more precious than your time and the fact that you dedicated some of yours with me is much appreciated. I hope that you were able to find some value from the hindsight of others as well as in the content I provided.

To Kendra and Brilynn - thanks for taking particular interest in the creation of this book. The check-ins, the nudges, the gifts, and encouragement did not go unnoticed and fueled me every time. Thank you for supporting me in this effort.

Mom, Tony, Taryn, Matt, Maria, Nick, and Lauren - thanks for being the best family out there. Your belief in all things I go after, not just this particular project, means more than you know.

Mike, my partner in life for the last few decades and all the decades to come. Thank you for sending me to my first writers' conference back in 2008. Thank you for allowing me all the time and space to work on this undertaking. Thank you for all the wine and coffee and yummy meals you've made for me, quite literally fueling this effort at all stages. But most of all, thank you for having an unwavering belief in me. I'm so glad I'll never know what it's like to be married to someone who isn't constantly in my corner, pushing the hardest and cheering the loudest.

And finally - DaD (he knows why the last D is capitalized). I have yet to meet - and know I never will - a man who has more love and admiration for his family. I am so honored to be part of the legacy that you've created and appreciate everything you do, even the things you don't think I see, for me and our entire family. You have so much faith in those you love and I know that once you get a copy of this book in your hands, you'll be "impressed...but not surprised." The smartest thing I've ever done in life is pick you to be my father.

With immense gratitude,

Alicia

BOOK RECOMMENDATIONS

PERSONAL FINANCE:

The Money Book for the Young, Broke and Fabulous - **Suze Orman**

The Money Book for the Young, Fabulous, & Broke is financial *expert Suze Orman's answer to a generation's cry for help. They're called "Generation Debt", people in their 20s and 30s who graduate from college with a mountain of student loan debt and are stuck with one of the weakest job markets in recent history, yet they're painfully aware of the urgent need to take matters into their own hands.*

The Money Book *was written to address the specific financial reality that young people face today. Suze Orman tells her young, fabulous, and broke listeners precisely what actions to take and why. Her advice at times bucks conventional wisdom (Did she just say use your credit card?) and may even seem counterintuitive (Pay into a retirement fund even though your credit card debt is killing you?), but it's her honesty, understanding, and uncanny ability to anticipate the needs of her readers that have made her the most trusted financial expert of the day.*

Suze takes listeners past broke, to a secure place where they'll never have to worry about revisiting broke again. And she begins the journey with a bit of overwhelmingly good news (yes, there really is good news): Young people have the greatest asset of all on their side - time.

The Total Money Makeover - **Dave Ramsey**

Okay, folks, do you want to turn those fat and flabby expenses into a well-toned budget? Do you want to transform your sad and skinny little bank account into a bulked-up cash machine? Then get with the program, people. There's one sure way to whip your finances into shape, and that's with The Total Money Makeover. *It's the simplest, most straight-forward game plan for completely making over your money habits. And it's based on results, not pie-in-the-sky fantasies.*

The Automatic Millionaire - **David Bach**

In The Automatic Millionaire, *David Bach shares the secret to becoming a millionaire.*

The Automatic Millionaire *starts with the powerful story of an average American couple (he's a low-level manager, she's a beautician), whose joint income never exceeds $55,000 a year, who somehow manage to own two homes debt-free, put two kids through college, and retire at 55 with more than $1 million in savings. Through their story you'll learn the surprising fact that you cannot get rich with a budget! You must have a plan to pay yourself that is totally automatic, a plan that will automatically secure your future and pay for your present.*

What Makes The Automatic Millionaire *unique:*

- *You don't need to make a lot of money*
- *You don't need a budget*
- *You don't need willpower*
- *You don't need to be that interested in money*

You can set up the plan in an hour. This one little audiobook has the power to secure your financial future. Do it once, the rest is automatic!

RESUME GUIDANCE:

How to Write the Perfect Resume - Dan Clay

Picture a scenario: You're sitting at your kitchen table scrolling through job listings when you see one that catches your eye. As you read through the job description, your excitement builds as you realize that the job is a perfect fit! Not wasting another second, you fill out the application, attach your resume, and hold your breath as you hit "Apply."

Then you wait. And wait. And wait some more. Weeks go by without hearing so much as a peep, and before long you've given up hope on what seemed like a match made in heaven.

Sound familiar? You're not alone! On average there are 250 resumes submitted for every job opening, which means that 99.6% of applicants will fail to land the jobs they apply for.

To get the job you want, you don't just need a great resume--you need an outstanding resume, one that puts you in the top 1% of candidates for the job. That means ditching the same old advice you've been following with little results and adopting a tried-and-true process for getting your resume noticed in even the most competitive situations.

In this book, Dan Clay breaks down the exact method he's carefully developed over a period of ten years and provides a precise, step-by-step set of instructions for crafting the perfect resume, down to the last period.

And when it comes to something as important as your career, don't you deserve to learn from someone who's actually succeeded at doing what you're hoping to do?

PLUS, you'll also gain access to a free companion website containing fully editable resume templates, a perfect resume checklist, and other bonus materials to give you everything you need to create a stunning resume that will get you noticed and land you interviews.

Whether you're a new graduate looking for your first job, a career veteran angling for your next move, a recent victim of a layoff, or someone looking to dip their toes back into the workplace after taking a few years off, this comprehensive guide aims to be the best--and last--resume writing book you'll ever need for your career.

Resumes for Dummies - **Laura DeCarlo**

We've all been there: it's time to apply for a job or internship and you have to create or revise your resume. Many questions pop in your head. What do employers want? What skills should I highlight? How do I format this? How do I get noticed? But resume writing doesn't have to be a daunting task.

The latest edition of Resumes For Dummies *answers all of these questions and more—whether you're a resume rookie, looking for new tips, or want to create that eye-catching winning resume. In this trusted guide, Laura DeCarlo decodes the modern culture of resume writing and offers you insider tips on all the best practices that'll make your skills shine and your resume pop. Let's start writing!*

- *Write effective resumes that will stand out in a crowd*
- *Understand Applicant Tracking Systems and how to adapt your resume*
- *Keep your resume up with the current culture*
- *Position a layoff or other career change and challenge with a positive spin*
- *Leverage tips and tricks that give your resume visual power*

In order to put your best foot forward and stand out in a pile of papers, it's important to have an excellent and effective resume—and now you can.

POSITIVE MINDSET:

Girl Wash Your Face - **Rachel Hollis**

Do you ever suspect that everyone else has life figured out and you don't have a clue? If so, Rachel Hollis has something to tell you: that's a lie.

If you have ever said any of these things to yourself... something else will make me happy; I'm not a good mom; I will never get past this; I am defined by my weight; I should be further along by now...then you could benefit from the unflinching faith and rock-hard tenacity Rachel Hollis has in store for you. In this challenging but conversational audiobook, Rachel exposes the 20 lies and misconceptions that too often hold us back from living joyfully and productively, lies we've told ourselves so often we don't even hear them anymore.

Rachel is real and talks about real issues. More than that, she reveals the specific practical strategies that helped her move past them. In the process, she encourages, entertains, and even kicks a little butt, all to convince you to do whatever it takes to get real and become the joyous, confident woman you were meant to be. Because you really can live with passion and hustle - and give yourself grace without giving up.

The 5 Second Rule - **Mel Robbins**

How to enrich your life and destroy doubt in five seconds.

Throughout your life, you've had parents, coaches, teachers, friends, and mentors who have pushed you to be better than your excuses and bigger than your fears. What if the secret to having the confidence and courage to enrich your life and work is simply knowing how to push yourself?

Using the science of habits, riveting stories, and surprising facts from some of the most famous moments in history, art, and business, Mel Robbins will explain the power of a "push moment". Then, she'll give you one simple tool you can use to become your greatest self.

It takes just five seconds to use this tool, and every time you do you'll be in great company. More than eight million people have watched Mel's TEDx Talk, and executives inside of the world's largest brands are using the tool to increase productivity, collaboration, and engagement.

In The 5 Second Rule, *you'll discover it takes just five seconds to:*

- *Become confident*
- *Break the habit of procrastination and self-doubt*
- *Beat fear and uncertainty*
- *Stop worrying and feel happier*
- *Share your ideas with courage*

The 5 Second Rule *is a simple, one-size-fits-all solution for the one problem we all face - we hold ourselves back. The secret isn't knowing what to do - it's knowing how to make yourself do it.*

Atomic Habits - James Clear

No matter your goals, Atomic Habits *offers a proven framework for improving - every day. James Clear, one of the world's leading experts on habit formation, reveals practical strategies that will teach you exactly how to form good habits, break bad ones, and master the tiny behaviors that lead to remarkable results.*

If you're having trouble changing your habits, the problem isn't you. The problem is your system. Bad habits repeat themselves again and again not because you don't want to change, but because you have the wrong system for change. You do not rise to the level of your goals. You fall to the level of your systems. Here, you'll get a proven system that can take you to new heights.

Clear is known for his ability to distill complex topics into simple behaviors that can be easily applied to daily life and work. Here, he draws on the most proven ideas from biology, psychology, and neuroscience to create an easy-to-understand guide for making good habits inevitable and bad habits impossible. Along the way, listeners will be inspired and entertained with true stories from Olympic gold medalists, award-winning artists, business leaders, life-saving physicians, and star comedians who have used the science of small habits to master their craft and vault to the top of their field. Learn how to:

- *make time for new habits (even when life gets crazy);*
- *overcome a lack of motivation and willpower;*
- *design your environment to make success easier;*
- *And get back on track when you fall off course*

Atomic Habits *will reshape the way you think about progress and success, and give you the tools and strategies you need to transform your habits - whether you are a team looking to win a championship, an organization hoping to redefine an industry, or simply an individual who wishes to quit smoking, lose weight, reduce stress, or achieve any other goal.*

You Are a Badass - Jen Sincero

Best-selling author, speaker, and world-traveling success coach Jen Sincero cuts through the din of the self-help genre with her own verbal meat cleaver in You Are a Badass: How to Stop Doubting Your Greatness and Start Living an Awesome Life. *In this refreshingly blunt how-to guide, Sincero serves up 27 bite-sized chapters full of hilariously inspiring stories, life-changing insights, easy exercises, and the occasional swear word.*

Via chapters such as "Your Brain Is Your Bitch", "Fear Is for Suckers", and "My Subconscious Made Me Do It", Sincero takes you on a wild joy ride to your own transformation, helping you create the money, relationships, career, and general all-around awesomeness you so desire. And should you be one of those people who dreads getting busted with a self-help book in your hands, fear not.

Sincero, a former skeptic herself, delivers the goods minus the New Age cheese, giving even the snarkiest of poo-pooers exactly what they need to get out of their ruts and start kicking some ass. By the end of You Are a Badass, *you will understand why you are how you are, how to love what you can't change, how to change what you don't love, and how to start living the kind of life you used to be jealous of.*

Extreme Ownership - Jocko Willink, Leif Babin

Combat, the most intense and dynamic environment imaginable, teaches the toughest leadership lessons, with absolutely everything at stake. Jocko Willink and Leif Babin learned this reality first-hand on the most violent and dangerous battlefield in Iraq. As leaders of SEAL Team Three's Task Unit Bruiser, their mission was one many thought impossible: help US forces secure Ramadi, a violent, insurgent-held city deemed "all but lost." In gripping, firsthand accounts of heroism, tragic loss, and hard-won victories, they learned that leadership - at every level - is the most important factor in whether a team succeeds or fails.

Willink and Babin returned home from deployment and instituted SEAL leadership training to pass on their harsh lessons learned in combat to help forge the next generation of SEAL leaders. After leaving the SEAL Teams, they launched a company, Echelon Front, to teach those same leadership principles to leaders in businesses, companies, and organizations across the civilian sector. Since that time, they have trained countless leaders and worked with hundreds of companies in virtually every industry across the US and internationally, teaching them how to develop their own high-performance teams and most effectively lead those teams to dominate their battlefields.

Since its release in October 2015, Extreme Ownership *has revolutionized leadership development and set a new standard for literature on the subject. Required reading for many of the most successful organizations, it has become an integral part of the official leadership training programs for scores of business teams, military units, and first responders. Detailing the mindset and principles that enable SEAL units to accomplish the most difficult combat missions,* Extreme Ownership *demonstrates how to apply them to any team or organization, in any leadership environment. A compelling narrative with powerful instruction and direct application,* Extreme Ownership *challenges leaders everywhere to fulfill their ultimate purpose: lead and win.*

GOAL SETTING:

The 10x Rule - Grant Cardone

Extreme success, by definition, lies beyond the realm of normal action. If you want to achieve extreme success, you can't operate like everybody else and settle for mediocrity. You need to remove luck and chance from your business equation, and lock in massive success. The 10X Rule shows you how! Success is your duty, obligation and responsibility, and this audio book gives you step-by-step guidance on how to achieve phenomenal success for yourself!

With The 10X Rule *, you'll learn to establish the amount of effort needed to guarantee success and ensure that you can continue operating at this level throughout your life. Most people desire success and have great ideas but they come up short on the amount of action required to get their lives to the exceptional levels they deserve. Four degrees of action exist, and in order to achieve your dreams, you must learn to operate at the fourth degree of action: Massive Action. The 10X Rule will dissolve fear, increase your belief in yourself, eliminate procrastination, and provide you with an overwhelming sense of purpose. The 10X Rule compels you to separate yourself from everyone else in the market—and you do that by doing* *what others refuse to do. Stop thinking in terms of basic needs, and start aiming for abundance—in all areas of your life. The 10X Rule guides you toward the frame of mind that all successful people share. Aim ten times higher than you are right now—and if you come up short, you'll still find yourself further along than if you had maintained your life's current status quo. The 10X Rule teaches you how to:*

- *Reach goals that you previously thought were impossible*
- *Correctly set goals and guarantee their achievement*
- *Create unprecedented levels of happiness and satisfaction in every area of your life*
- *Use fear as fuel to move you into action*
- *Get everything you want and never have to settle*
- *Dominate your competition and become a role model for success*

Finish - Jon Acuff

Jon Acuff, sought-after speaker and consultant, is the friend who always gives you great advice. With his self-deprecating humor and charm, he has won over hundreds of thousands of followers who come to him for both encouragement and a kick in the pants. Now, after showing you how to reboot your career in his New York Times best seller Do Over, Acuff shows chronic starters how to actually finish their goals in an age of bottomless distractions and endless opportunities.

Acuff knows the reason why many writers' novels go unfinished - it's the same reason why gyms are filled in the first week of January and empty by the end of the month and why people stop learning a new language once they get past the easy parts. It's not just that people lose momentum or get distracted. People give up on projects when they fail to live up to their own high expectations and decide that if they can't do something perfectly, they won't do it at all. If you're going to finish, you have to kill perfectionism.

Drawing on his popular 30 Days of Hustle course, Acuff teaches listeners to short-circuit perfectionism and make it through to the end of a task. Whether it's by "choosing what to bomb" or "cutting a goal in half", he shows listeners how to move past "the day after perfect", get focused, and - finally - finish.

The Compound Effect - **Darren Hardy**

The Compound Effect *contains the essence of what every super achiever needs to know, practice, and master to obtain extraordinary success. Inside you will hear strategies on:*

- *How to win-every time*
- *Eradicating the bad habits that are derailing your progress*
- *Painlessly installing the few key disciplines required for major breakthroughs*
- *The real, lasting keys to gaining and sustaining motivation*
- *Capturing the elusive, awesome force of momentum*
- *The acceleration secrets of superachievers*

Inside you will learn how to get the success you desire and the life you deserve.

NETWORK MARKETING:

Miracle Morning for Network Marketers - **Hal Elrod, Pat Petrini, Honorée Corder**

Tried all the networking marketing tricks without results? It's time to transform your daily routine and grow yourself first to grow your business fast!

You've consumed all the books on sales techniques, generating leads, and closing, but you aren't making the progress you'd hoped for. What if you could make a few simple changes to increase your income, reduce your stress, and send your fulfillment through the roof? Start the next chapter of your career with a system that's been time tested by hundreds of thousands of people worldwide.

The Miracle Morning for Network Marketers *uses Hal Elrod's global phenomenon to give you the strategies, mindset, and daily rituals that match the top 1 percent of all network marketers, so you can grow yourself and your business faster than you ever thought possible.*

Once you've nailed down your miracle morning, Hal Elrod and Pat Petrini's book shows you exactly what you should be doing with "the rest of your day". When you apply these fundamental business building skills to your network marketing business, you won't just get to the top...you'll stay there.

The Miracle Morning for Network Marketers *is your key to making immediate and profound changes on the path to a bigger team and the life of your dreams. Listen now to discover the simplest, fastest path to network marketing prosperity.*

Go Pro - by Eric Worre

Over twenty years ago at a company convention, Eric Worre had an "aha" moment that changed his life forever. At that event he made the decision to Go Pro *and become a Network Marketing expert. Since that time, he has focused on developing the skills to do just that. In doing so, Eric has touched and been touched by hundreds of thousands of people around the world. Now he shares his wisdom in a guide that will ignite your passion for this profession and help you make the decision to Go Pro and create the life of your dreams.*

In this definitive guidebook, you will learn to:

- *Find prospects*
- *Invite them to your product or opportunity*
- *Present your product*
- *Follow up with your prospects*
- *Help them become customers or distributors*
- *Help them get started right*
- *Grow your team by promoting events*
- *And much, much more...*

Eric s wish is for you to make the decision to become a Network Marketing Professional. For you to truly Go Pro. Because it is a stone-cold fact that Network Marketing is a better way. Now let's go tell the world.

DEALING WITH PERSONAL LOSS/FAILURE:

Option B - Sheryl Sandberg

From Facebook's COO and Wharton's top-rated professor, the number-one New York Times best-selling authors of Lean In and Originals: a powerful, inspiring, and practical book about building resilience and moving forward after life's inevitable setbacks.

After the sudden death of her husband, Sheryl Sandberg felt certain that she and her children would never feel pure joy again. "I was in 'the void,'" she writes, "a vast emptiness that fills your heart and lungs and restricts your ability to think or even breathe." Her friend Adam Grant, a psychologist at Wharton, told her there are concrete steps people can take to recover and rebound from life-shattering experiences. We are not born with a fixed amount of resilience. It is a muscle that everyone can build.

Option B combines Sheryl's personal insights with Adam's eye-opening research on finding strength in the face of adversity. Beginning with the gut-wrenching moment when she finds her husband, Dave Goldberg, collapsed on a gym floor, Sheryl opens up her heart - and her journal - to describe the acute grief and isolation she felt in the wake of his death. But Option B goes beyond Sheryl's loss to explore how a broad range of people have overcome hardships including illness, job loss, sexual assault, natural disasters, and the violence of war. Their stories reveal the capacity of the human spirit to persevere...and to rediscover joy.

Resilience comes from deep within us and from support outside us. Even after the most devastating events, it is possible to grow by finding deeper meaning and gaining greater appreciation in our lives. Option B Illuminates how to help others in crisis, develop compassion for ourselves, raise strong children, and create resilient families, communities, and workplaces. Many of these lessons can be applied to everyday struggles, allowing us to brave whatever lies ahead.

Two weeks after losing her husband, Sheryl was preparing for a father-child activity. "I want Dave," she cried. Her friend replied, "Option A is not available," and then promised to help her make the most of Option B.

We all live some form of Option B. This book will help us all make the most of it.

The Gifts of Imperfection - **Brene Brown**

For over a decade, Brené Brown has found a special place in our hearts as a gifted mapmaker and a fellow traveler. She is both a social scientist and a kitchen table friend whom you can always count on to tell the truth, make you laugh, and, on occasion, cry with you. And what's now become a movement *all started with* The Gifts of Imperfection, *which has sold over two million copies in 35 different languages across the globe.*

What transforms this book from words to effective daily practices are the 10 guideposts to wholehearted living. The guideposts not only help us understand the practices that will allow us to change our lives and families, they also walk us through the unattainable and sabotaging expectations that get in the way.

Brené writes, "This book is an invitation to join a wholehearted revolution. A small, quiet, grassroots movement that starts with each of us saying, 'My story matters because I matter.' Revolution might sound a little dramatic, but in this world, choosing authenticity and worthiness is an absolute act of resistance."

Failing Forward - John C. Maxwell

The major difference between achieving people and average people is their perception of and response to failure. John C. Maxwell takes a closer look at failure - and reveals that the secret of moving beyond failure is to use it as a lesson and a stepping-stone. He covers the top reasons people fail and shows how to master fear instead of being mastered by it. Listeners will discover that positive benefits can accompany negative experiences - if you have the right attitude.

Chock full of action suggestions and real-life stores, Failing Forward is a strategic guide that will help men and women move beyond mistakes to fulfill their potential and achieve success.

APPENDIX

"Job Prospects for New College Grads Abound, According to New Survey," CareerBuilder, 2018, https://www.careerbuilder.com/advice/job-prospects-for-new-college-grads-abound-according-to-a-new-survey

"Everything You Need to Know About Landing a New Job This Year," CareerBuilder, 2019, https://www.careerbuilder.com/advice/everything-you-need-to-know-about-landing-a-new-job-this-year

"The Class of 2018 Career Report," LendEDU, 2018, https://lendedu.com/blog/career-report-class-of-2018/

"Percentage of Recent College Graduates in the United States who are Underemployed as of February 2019, by Major," Statista, https://www.statista.com/statistics/642226/underemployment-rate-of-us-college-graduates-by-major/

"Student Loan Debt Statistics In 2019: A $1.5 Trillion Crisis," *Forbes*, 2019, https://www.forbes.com/sites/zackfriedman/2019/02/25/student-loan-debt-statistics-2019/#d6da9d9133fb

https://investmentmoats.com/investment-advice/richard-russells-wisdom-rich-man-poor-man/

SAMPLE CREDIT REPORT

Sample Credit Report | Free Annual Credit Report | Experian Credit Report | Experian Credit Score

Experian
A world of insight

Online Personal Credit Report from Experian for

Experian credit report prepared for
JOHN Q CONSUMER
Your report number is
1562064065
Report date:
04/24/2012

Index:
- Potentially negative items
- Accounts in good standing
- Requests for your credit history
- Personal information
- Important message from Experian
- Contact us

Report number:

You will need your report number to contact Experian online, by phone or by mail.

Index:

Navigate through the sections of your credit report using these links.

Experian collects and organizes information about you and your credit history from public records, your creditors and other reliable sources. Experian makes your credit history available to your current and prospective creditors, employers and others as allowed by law, which can expedite your ability to obtain credit and can make offers of credit available to you. We do not grant or deny credit; each credit grantor makes that decision based on its own guidelines.

To return to your report in the near future, log on to www..experian.com/consumer and select "View your report again" or "Dispute" and then enter your report number.

If you disagree with information in this report, return to the Report Summary page and follow the instructions for disputing.

Potentially Negative Items

Public Records

Credit grantors may carefully review the items listed below when they check your credit history. Please note that the account information connected with some public records, such as bankruptcy, also may appear with your credit items listed later in this report.

MAIN COUNTY CLERK

Address:	Identification Number:	Plaintiff:
123 MAINTOWN S	1	ANY COMMISSIONER O.
BUFFALO , NY 10000		

Status:	Status Details:
Civil claim paid.	This item was verified and updated in Apr 2012.

Date Filed:	Claim Amount:
10/15/2012	$200
Date Resolved:	Liability
03/04/2012	Amount:
	NA
Responsibility:	
INDIVIDUAL	

Potentially negative items:

Items that creditors may view less favorably. It includes the creditor's name and address, your account number (shortened for security), account status, type and terms of the account and any other information reported to Experian by the creditor. Also includes any bankruptcy, lien and judgment information obtained directly from the courts.

Status:

Indicates the current status of the account.

Credit Items

For your protection, the last few digits of your account numbers do not display.

ABCD BANKS

Address:	Account Number:
100 CENTER RD	1000000....
BUFFALO, NY 10000	
(555) 555-5555	
Status: Paid/Past due 60 days.	

Date Opened:	Type:	Credit Limit/Original Amount:
10/2012	Installment	$523
Reported Since:	Terms:	High Balance:
11/2012	12 Months	NA
Date of Status:	Monthly	Recent Balance:
04/2012	Payment:	$0 as of 04/2012
	$0	Recent Payment:
Last Reported:	Responsibility:	$0
04/2012	Individual	

Account History:
60 days as of 12-2012
30 days as of 11-2012

If you believe information in your report is inaccurate, you can dispute that item quickly, effectively and cost free by using Experian's online dispute service located at:

www.experian.com/disputes

Disputing online is the fastest way to address any concern you may have about the information in your credit report.

MAIN COLL AGENCIES

Address:	Account Number:	Original Creditor:
PO BOX 123	0123456789	TELEVISE CABLE COMM.
ANYTOWN, PA 10000		
(555) 555-5555		

Status: Collection account. $95 past due as of 4-2012.

Date Opened:	Type:	Credit Limit/Original Amount:
01/2005	Installment	$95
Reported Since:	Terms:	High Balance:
04/2012	NA	NA
Date of Status:	Monthly	Recent Balance:
04/2012	Payment:	$95 as of 04/2012
	$0	Recent Payment:
Last Reported:	Responsibility:	$0
04/2012	Individual	

Your statement: ITEM DISPUTED BY CONSUMER

Account History:
Collection as of 4-2012

Accounts in Good Standing   **5**

Accounts in good standing:

Lists accounts that have a positive status and may be viewed favorably by creditors. Some creditors do not report to us, so some of your accounts may not be listed.

AUTOMOBILE AUTO FINANCE

Address:	Account Number:
100 MAIN ST E	12345678998....
SMALLTOWN, MD 90001	
(555) 555-5555	

Status: Open/Never late.

Date Opened:	Type:	Credit Limit/Original Amount:
01/2006	Installment **6**	$10,355
Reported Since:	Terms:	High Balance:
01/2012	65 Months	NA
Date of Status:	Monthly	Recent Balance:
04/2012	Payment:	$7,984 as of 04/2012
	$210	Recent Payment:
Last Reported:	Responsibility:	$0
04/2012	Individual	

Type:

Account type indicates whether your account is a revolving or an installment account.

MAIN

Address:	Account Number:
PO BOX 1234	1234567899876
FORT LAUDERDALE, FL 10009	

Status: Closed/Never late.

Date Opened:	Type:	Credit Limit/Original Amount:
03/1997	Revolving	NA
Reported Since:	Terms:	High Balance:
03/2012	1 Months	$3,228
Date of Status:	Monthly	Recent Balance:
08/2012	Payment:	$0 /paid as of 08/2012
	$0	Recent Payment:
Last Reported:	Responsibility:	$0
08/2012	Individual	

Your statement:
Account closed at consumer's request

Requests for Your Credit History   `7`

Requests Viewed By Others

We make your credit history available to your current and prospective creditors and employers as allowed by law. Personal data about you may be made available to companies whose products and services may interest you.

The section below lists all who have requested in the recent past to review your credit history as a result of actions involving you, such as the completion of a credit application or the transfer of an account to a collection agency, application for insurance, mortgage or loan application, etc. Creditors may view these requests when evaluating your creditworthiness.

HOMESALE REALTY CO

Address:	Date of Request:
2000 S MAINROAD BLVD STE	07/16/2012
ANYTOWN CA 11111	
(555) 555-5555	

Comments:
Real estate loan on behalf of 3903 MERCHANTS EXPRESS M. This inquiry is scheduled to continue on record until 8-2014.

M & T BANK

Address:	Date of Request:
PO BOX 100	02/23/2006
BUFFALO NY 10000	
(555) 555-5555	

Comments:
Permissible purpose. This inquiry is scheduled to continue on record until 3-2008.

WESTERN FUNDING INC

Address:	Date of Request:
191 W MAIN AVE STE 100	01/25/2006
INTOWN CA 10000	
(555) 555-5555	

Comments:
Permissible purpose. This inquiry is scheduled to continue on record until 2-2008.

Requests Viewed Only By You

The section below lists all who have a permissible purpose by law and have requested in the recent past to review your information. You may not have initiated these requests, so you may not recognize each source. We offer information about you to those with a permissible purpose, for example, to:

- other creditors who want to offer you preapproved credit;
- an employer who wishes to extend an offer of employment;
- a potential investor in assessing the risk of a current obligation;
- Experian or other credit reporting agencies to process a report for you;
- your existing creditors to monitor your credit activity (date listed may reflect only the most recent request).

We report these requests **only to you** as a record of activities. We **do not** provide this information to other creditors who evaluate your creditworthiness.

MAIN BANK USA

Address:	Date of Request:
1 MAIN CTR AA 11	08/10/2012
BUFFALO NY 14203	

MYTOWN BANK

Address:	Date of Request:
PO BOX 825	08/05/2006
MYTOWN DE 10000	
(555) 555-5555	

INTOWN DATA CORPS

Address:	Date of Request:
2000 S MAINTOWN BLVD STE	07/16/2006
INTOWN CO 11111	
(555) 555-5555	

Requests for your credit history:

Also called "inquiries," requests for your credit history are logged on your report whenever anyone reviews your credit information. There are two types of inquiries.

i.
Inquiries resulting from a transaction initiated by you. These include inquiries from your applications for credit, insurance, housing or other loans. They also include transfer of an account to a collection agency. Creditors may view these items when evaluating your creditworthiness.

ii.
Inquiries resulting from transactions you may not have initiated but that are allowed under the FCRA. These include preapproved offers, as well as for employment, investment review, account monitoring by existing creditors, and requests by you for your own report. These items are shown only to you and have no impact on your creditworthiness or risk scores.

Personal Information **8**

The following information is reported to us by you, your creditors and other sources. Each source may report your personal information differently, which may result in variations of your name, address, Social Security number, etc. As part of our fraud prevention efforts, a notice with additional information may appear. As a security precaution, the Social Security number that you used to obtain this report is not displayed. The Name identification number and Address identification number are how our system identifies variations of your name and address that may appear on your report. The Geographical Code shown with each address identifies the state, county, census tract, block group and Metropolitan Statistical Area associated with each address.

Names:
JOHN Q CONSUMER
Name identification number: 15621

JONATHON Q CONSUMER
Name identification number: 15622

J Q CONSUMER
Name identification number: 15623

Social Security number variations:
999999999

Year of birth:
1959

Spouse or co-applicant:
JANE

Employers:
ABCDE ENGINEERING CORP

Telephone numbers:
(555) 555 5555 Residential

Address: 123 MAIN STREET
ANYTOWN, MD 90001-9999
Address identification number:
0277741504
Type of Residence: Multifamily
Geographical Code: 0-156510-31-8840 **9**

Address: 555 SIMPLE PLACE
ANYTOWN, MD 90002-7777
Address identification number:
0170086050
Type of Residence: Single family
Geographical Code: 0-176510-33-8840

Address: 999 HIGH DRIVE APT 15B
ANYTOWN, MD 90003-5555
Address identification number:
0170129301
Type of Residence: Apartment complex
Geographical Code: 0-156510-31-8840

Your Personal Statement **10**

No general personal statements appear on your report.

Important Message From Experian

By law, we cannot disclose certain medical information (relating to physical, mental, or behavioral health or condition). Although we do not generally collect such information, it could appear in the name of a data furnisher (i.e., "Cancer Center") that reports your payment history to us. If so, those names display in your report, but in reports to others they display only as MEDICAL PAYMENT DATA. Consumer statements included on your report at your request that contain medical information are disclosed to others.

Contacting Us

Contact address and phone number for your area will display here.

©Experian 2012. All rights reserved.
Experian and the Experian marks herein are service marks or registered trademarks of Experian.

Personal information: Personal information associated with your history that has been reported to Experian by you, your creditors and other sources.

May include name and Social Security number variations, employers, telephone numbers, etc. Experian lists all variations so you know what is being reported to us as belonging to you.

Address information: Your current address and previous address(es)

Personal statement: Any personal statement that you added to your report appears here.

Note - statements remain as part of the report for two years and display to anyone who has permission to review your report.